"Despite its title, readers should not come to *Finally Feminist* with expectations of any final, watertight answer to the gender debate. A practical theologian, Stackhouse considers both complementarian and egalitarian views of women's roles and comes up with a paradigm that is evenhanded, orthodox, contemporary, and temporary. That is, he uses historical and eschatological lenses to look to both the past and the future to form a realistic model for Christian men and women in the present."

—**Luci Shaw,** writer in residence, Regent College; author of *The Crime of Living Cautiously*

"Changing one's mind about the gender question often requires a dramatic paradigm shift, a new model for thinking about things. Unveiling key moments within his own change of mind, Stackhouse calls the Christian community to think about and rethink the way we understand biblical texts about gender, especially when people on both sides of the debate, given a certain selectivity of texts, can happily exegete their way to either egalitarian or patriarchal conclusions. The book's proposed paradigm of 'double meaning' and 'holy pragmatism' within Scripture holds implications and challenges for both sides to ponder. This is a powerful and personal book, well worth the reading. Let us listen carefully, and let the community discussion continue."

—**William J. Webb,** author of *Slaves, Women, and Homosexuals*

"This book invites both sides of the gender roles debate to the table afresh. I like that no one is particularly at ease here and no one's view is accepted without challenge. Stackhouse suggests that this discomfort might be worthwhile for everyone. As we all grapple with how to be ourselves in a complex world, this book offers important insights and reflections to both men and women and to both conservatives and liberals."

—**Allyson Jule,** senior lecturer in education, University of Glamorgan

Finally Feminist

Acadia Studies in Bible and Theology

Craig A. Evans and Lee Martin McDonald, General Editors

The last two decades have witnessed dramatic developments in biblical and theological study. Full-time academics can scarcely keep up with fresh discoveries, recently published primary texts, ongoing archaeological work, new exegetical proposals, experiments in methods and hermeneutics, and innovative theological syntheses. For students and nonspecialists, these developments are confusing and daunting. What has been needed is a series of succinct studies that assess these issues and present their findings in a way that students, pastors, laity, and nonspecialists will find accessible and rewarding. Acadia Studies in Bible and Theology, sponsored by Acadia Divinity College in Wolfville, Nova Scotia, and in conjunction with the college's Hayward Lectureship, constitutes such a series.

The Hayward Lectureship has brought to Acadia many distinguished scholars of Bible and theology, such as Sir Robin Barbour, John Bright, Leander Keck, Helmut Koester, Richard Longenecker, Martin Marty, Jaroslav Pelikan, Ian Rennie, James Sanders, and Eduard Schweizer. The Acadia Studies in Bible and Theology series reflects this rich heritage.

These studies are designed to guide readers through the ever more complicated maze of critical, interpretative, and theological discussion taking place today. But these studies are not introductory in nature; nor are they mere surveys. Authored by leading authorities in the field, the Acadia Studies in Bible and Theology series offers critical assessments of the major issues that the church faces in the twenty-first century. Readers will gain the requisite orientation and fresh understanding of the important issues that will enable them to take part meaningfully in discussion and debate.

Finally Feminist

A Pragmatic
Christian Understanding of Gender

John G. Stackhouse, Jr.

Baker Academic
Grand Rapids, Michigan

Published by Baker Academic
a division of Baker Publishing Group
P.O. Box 6287, Grand Rapids, MI 49516-6287
www.bakeracademic.com

Printed in the United States of America

Library of Congress Cataloging-in-Publication Data
Stackhouse, John Gordon.
    Finally feminist : a pragmatic Christian understanding of gender / John G. Stackhouse, Jr.
       p. cm. — (Acadia studies in Bible and theology)
    Includes bibliographical references and index.
    ISBN 0-8010-3130-3 (pbk.)
    1. Sex role—Religious aspects—Christianity. I. Title. II. Series.
BT708.S67 2006
270′.082—dc22   2005014107

To
Aunt Donna-Jean,
Aunt Jan,
Aunt Val,
and Kari

Contents

Preface   9

1 Toward a New Paradigm   15
2 The Paradigm   33
3 Responses to Arguments   75

Appendix A: How *Not* to Decide about Gender   105
Appendix B: A Woman's Place Is in . . . Theology?   115
Subject Index   131
Scripture Index   137

Preface

Aren't we "done" with gender? Haven't all the relevant issues been raised, all the texts scrutinized, all the alternatives arrayed?

Christian discussion regarding the identity and roles of men and women typically has been conducted between two sorts of Christians: those who side with the tradition of patriarchy, in one form or another, and those who identify with some sort of feminism. Since the middle of the nineteenth century, the voices of preachers, theologians, exegetes, activists, missionaries, and, latterly, social scientists have contributed to this vexed debate. These voices have been both male and female. Moreover, and perhaps surprisingly to some, male and female voices have been heard on both sides: Not all patriarchalists have been male, nor have all feminists been women. Furthermore, neither side has demonstrated a corner on piety, orthodoxy, fidelity, or charity. Nor can only one side command the fields of Scripture, theology, tradition, social science, and everyday experience. It seems abundantly evident that there are very good reasons to hold to either side of this debate. So is there anything left to say?

I want to address this issue as one who enjoys friends on both sides of this controversy. One of the ways in which this book perhaps offers something unusual in this discussion stems from my disposition to believe that *both sides are right*, for it seems unlikely to me that the intelligent and godly people who are found on one side or the other are totally, or even mostly, mistaken. (This point is rarely acknowledged by the polemicists, but many people in the pews—who often feel torn in their allegiances to friends on both sides—see it readily enough.) If a way can be found to hear each side fairly, to acknowledge not only the personal integrity of the participants but also the spiritual and intellectual integrity of their positions, then that way deserves a good look. It is that way I have chosen to take.

I have concluded also, however, that neither side's characteristic line of argumentation is entirely right. Hence, I here set forth a way of looking at gender that can affirm much, even most, of what both sides typically say and yet does so in what I hope is a single, coherent paradigm that amounts finally to a Christian feminism.

I do not claim uniqueness for this approach. In fact, I am rather leery of all claims of intellectual uniqueness, not only because they are usually impossible to prove (how can you know that no one has anticipated your ideas?) but also because they are suspiciously self-aggrandizing (why would God have vouchsafed such insights specially to you?). But I write this book because I have not seen quite this arrangement of ideas before. And it is this arrangement—and not the constituent particular arguments, most of which I have gratefully gathered from others—that has helped me most in thinking about this debate and is therefore this book's central contribution to that debate.[1]

This volume was occasioned by invitations in 2004 to give lectures at two North American evangelical schools: the Visiting Christian Scholar Lectures at Taylor University in Indiana

---

1. Auditors of my lectures on this subject have noted the resemblance of my paradigm to that offered in William J. Webb, *Slaves, Women, and Homosexuals* (Downers Grove, IL: InterVarsity, 2001). The "redemptive-movement hermeneutic" outlined by Webb is, indeed, similar. It suggests that in a wide range of issues, of which slavery and gender are chief examples, God first brings amelioration of a bad situation (oppression of foreigners and debtors, or of women), thus setting his people on a trajectory of redemption. The explicit ethical principles and injunctions of the Bible are a "step in the right direction" (my phrase, not

and the Hayward Lectures at Acadia Divinity College in Nova Scotia. Because I continue to worship and serve within evangelical Protestantism, I thought it well to speak to what is indeed a live and contentious issue in those ranks, however otiose it may seem in others. Moreover, it is clear that gender controversies continue to roil not only evangelical communities but also many communities elsewhere within Protestant Christianity, as well as in Roman Catholic and Eastern Orthodox circles—in North America and around the globe.

In the limited time such lectureships allow, and now in this small book, I have focused on the questions that are most controverted in most of these groups: the status and roles of women and men in church and family. There is, of course, much more to be said about gender. Kendall Cox lists other important items still on the larger agenda:

Webb's). We modern Christians are to understand that we now are to continue to walk in the right direction to fuller and fuller realizations of the redemption initiated in the biblical codes. Webb notes that "not everything within Scripture reflects the same level of ethical development" (41), and his approach is thus a dynamic one, over against a "static" one (his term) that tends to view biblical passages on gender as timelessly both true and directly relevant to all of God's people in every circumstance. As the Bible itself shows some "movement," so we are to extend that movement toward full redemption.

My contribution to this discussion is to clarify what Webb leaves at least occasionally unclear, namely, what it means to discern the spirit versus the words of the biblical text. Webb defends himself against too stark a distinction between these terms: "These two components are *not* antithetical; the words and spirit are fused together in the original text" (34). With that I agree. But I prefer to make clear that we do not need to distinguish the spirit from the words at all—not least because this sort of distinction is vulnerable to all sorts of abuse. Who is to say what the spirit is, if it is not interpreted from the words? And how do we arbitrate among competing interpretations of spirit? I fear any interpretation of the Bible that is not tethered at every vital point to the text.

So I make a different sort of distinction. Careful reading of the text itself, in my view, shows us a *double*, not a single, message. We see an affirmation of the equality of men and women that should issue eventually in the abolition of patriarchy. Yet we also see a temporary and culturally conditional accommodation to patriarchy pending the changed social circumstances in which patriarchy can be done away. Rather than having to appeal to the spirit of the text, then, I prefer a hermeneutic that simply tries to interpret all the relevant texts as coherently as possible. And, I should say, in *practice*, that is what I think Webb usually does in his useful book.

the sexualization of youth in advertisement; the impact of the "single breadwinner" economic system on middle-class men; dualism, sexual repression, and disembodied rationality; sexual objectification in the media; the correlation between child sexual abuse and authoritarianism in Christian households; the treatment of singles as second-class Christians; female complicity in their own subordination; the correlation between male pornography use and sexually violent attitudes toward women; the devaluing of emotion and relationship in masculine conditioning; suppression of stereotypically "feminine" attributes in men and stereotypically "masculine" attributes in women; rampant misandry and misogyny, etc.[2]

I trust, then, that this volume will contribute at least a little to the opening up of a wider range of conversations among evangelicals and also among the many other Christians who share these interests. In particular, I hope it will assist those who genuinely would like to become egalitarians but who cannot see how the Bible supports such a view. I also hope it will assist Christian feminists who might find at least some of the ideas in this book new and useful in their—our—cause.

Many other people come at this question, however, from a different angle. They are already feminists and wonder how they can have anything to do with an apparently sexist Bible full of "texts of terror" and other impediments to women.[3] I sympathize with these sisters and brothers. Biblical landscapes can often appear quite dangerous for women. To these friends also, then, I hope this book will be of service. I have come to believe that feminists do not need to censor the Bible, seek to excuse it, or cleverly circumvent it, much less abandon it. I have concluded

2. Kendall Cox, "Gender Matters: Supplement Your Education," *Et Cetera* (February 10, 2004): 1, 3. Indeed, Elaine Storkey shows that feminists argue among themselves as to the relative value of various items on the agenda: "What is the point of lengthy analyses of women's 'subjective inner space' when women's 'public external space' is still vulnerable to violence, rape, and attack? Why waste precious time with erudite articles on 'sites of jouissance' when so many women are still struggling with sites of poverty, single parenthood, or inadequate health resources?" (Elaine Storkey, *Origins of Difference: The Gender Debate Revisited* [Grand Rapids: Baker Academic, 2001], 62).

3. Phyllis Trible, *Texts of Terror: Literary-Feminist Readings of Biblical Narratives* (Philadelphia: Fortress, 1984).

instead that if we read it well—and *all* of it—then we can see that
the Bible does indeed speak "good news" to women, despite the
horrors it records and the evils it appears to condone.

I want to thank my hosts at the two institutions mentioned,
especially Daniel Bowell at Taylor and Craig Evans at Acadia.[4] My
editors at Baker Academic spurred me on to better work than I
would have done on my own: thanks to Jim Kinney and Melinda
Timmer in particular. The following friends graciously provided
a critical reading of some or all of the manuscript: Allyson Jule,
Jennie McLaurin, Cherith Fee Nordling, and Robert Yarbrough.
I am also grateful for the research assistance of Allison Kern and
Jennie McLaurin. And Elaine Yu compiled the index.

Finally, I dedicate this book to the beloved women who have
taught me the most on these matters, as on many others.

---

4. While at Acadia, theologian Jonathan Wilson asked me about my book's
relation to John Howard Yoder, *The Politics of Jesus* (Grand Rapids: Eerdmans,
1972), especially chap. 9, "Revolutionary Subordination," 163–92. John Howard
Yoder's reflections on this question doubtless shaped my thinking along the
way, encountering them as I did more than two decades ago. Yoder makes a
number of points with which I agree, and I will not cite them all here. Instead,
I will simply note that Yoder is an Anabaptist and I am an evangelical and will
remark that this difference makes a difference for the gender question too. We
both agree that Christians should participate in the *imitatio Christi* (the imitation
of Christ) and the *missio Christi* (the mission of Christ). We both agree that in
Christ men and women are equally valued, gifted, and employed. And we both
agree that women typically have been called on by God to exercise their freedom
and dignity in Christ by voluntarily subordinating themselves to their husbands,
male church leaders, and other forms of patriarchy in society at large. (I will
defend this apparently antifeminist position at length below.) Where we differ
is in emphasis: I emphasize the pragmatics of the situation (the *missio*) more
than does Yoder, who recognizes them but emphasizes the call to live like Christ
(the *imitatio*). (Cf. Willard M. Swartley's discussion of the tension between the
"pilgrim principle" and the "missionary principle" in his useful book *Slavery,
Sabbath, War, and Women: Case Issues in Biblical Interpretation* [Scottdale, PA:
Herald, 1983].) Yoder also does not press, as I do, for the eradication of patriarchy
in our churches and marriages today. My guess is that this difference between
us simply reflects the difference in North American society between the time of
his writing (the early 1970s) and the time of mine (some three decades later).
The abolition of patriarchy, which was not on the horizon then and therefore
was not to be sought by the "revolutionarily subordinate" Christian, is now a
broadly accepted social fact.

1

Toward a New Paradigm

The Problem

How can one be a Christian feminist?

For many people, "Christian feminist" is a contradiction in terms. Christians are supposed to believe in patriarchy—in male leadership in church and home, if not also in society at large. And most Christians have, in fact, so believed—regardless of age, race, class, or gender, across hundreds of cultures and two thousand years. Most Christians still believe in patriarchy, for the majority of Christians live outside the so-called developed countries in which feminism has made some important inroads. It is obvious, furthermore, that within those developed countries—and perhaps conspicuously in the largest and most influential of these, the United States of America—many Christians of almost every denominational stripe continue to believe that the Bible and Christian tradition are best understood as advocating the

submission of women to the authority of men at least in home
and church.

For its part, feminism, in the minds of many of these Christians, has been related to a wide range of social pathologies.
Feminism has been implicated in the so-called sexual liberation of women—in terms of both liberal mores (women are
free to be as promiscuous as men have been) and controversial
reproductive technologies (the Pill and the ready availability
of abortion). Feminism has been coupled with radical changes
in the public workplace that have brought many women into
jobs outside the home, including jobs previously dominated
by men. This availability of female labor has been blamed for
the depression of wages and the loss of benefits in many occupations that previously paid a "living wage" for a man and
his family. Feminism has been held responsible for children
having to go to day care or to let themselves in to their homes
in the afternoon with their "latchkeys" because both parents are
working outside the home—or, worse, because the parents are
divorced and the single parent is still at work. Feminism has
been associated with lesbianism and misanthropy—so much
so that many young women refuse to identify themselves as
feminists for fear they will be labeled "man haters." And feminism has been linked to hatred of the Christian church and its
Scriptures, as feminists have traced the oppression of women in
our culture particularly to the patriarchy endorsed by Christian
teaching throughout the ages.

So "Christian feminist" seems to many people to be the
"square circle" of our time. The suggestion of linking "Christian" and "feminist" strikes many contemporaries as both intellectually preposterous and morally outrageous—from both a
traditional Christian and a radical feminist point of view.

I respond to this situation from two, apparently opposed,
directions. On the one hand, I am a white, middle-class, heterosexual, evangelical Christian man—and thus clearly not
everyone's idea of a feminist. Indeed, one might think that I
would have a lot to lose in supporting the equal treatment of
women in every sphere of life—whether one sees that loss as
"legitimate authority" or "scandalous privilege." On the other

hand, I am also a career academician, someone who has earned degrees from two secular universities, has held appointments at three more, and has had books published by the presses of yet two others. Someone with that sort of mainstream scholarly background can be expected to be a feminist, of course. But one might not expect such a person to be an orthodox Bible believer.

In this book, then, I try to show how one can be both authentically feminist and authentically Christian. In particular, I try to show how the Bible, which has often been understood by *both* feminists and patriarchalists to be inimical to feminism, properly can be seen to support feminism in our time.[1]

The noun *feminist* can mean several things, but this is what I mean by it: someone who champions the dignity, rights, responsibilities, and glories of women as equal in importance to those of men and who therefore refuses discrimination against women. Thus, in this book, *feminist* and *egalitarian* are synonyms. Yes, women and men are biologically different, and so some sex-specific zones are real and therefore not arbitrary.[2] I expect that the folk wisdom is true that men and women differ also in other essential ways, although there is currently nothing approaching a cultural consensus as to what those ways are. Feminists, then, do not have to be blind to real differences and their implications. In fact, many feminists emphasize that women and men are indeed different and that a large part of the feminist concern is that those differences be acknowledged

1. Sandra Schneiders speaks for many feminist readers of Scripture: "Whereas the Bible permits a fairly straightforward connection between the oppression of the poor and the stranger in the biblical story and analogous oppression of the poor and racial-ethnic minorities in contemporary society, the biblical text is not only frequently blind to the oppression of women in the Israelite and early Christian communities, but the text itself is pervasively androcentric and patriarchal, frequently sexist, and even misogynist" (Sandra M. Schneiders, *The Revelatory Text: Interpreting the New Testament as Sacred Scripture* [San Francisco: Harper, 1991], 181–82).

2. It is apparent already that I am using the now-common distinction between "gender" (as the idea of what constitutes masculine and feminine in a given society or discourse) and "sex" (the biological distinction between male and female). To what extent, if any, gender and sex are actually, or "essentially," linked is a vexed theme of discussion in natural science, social science, philosophy, and theology.

and incorporated into our life together.[3] Feminists of the sort I represent are those who resist what they judge to be *arbitrary, ungrounded* distinctions between men and women and the discrimination that attends such distinctions.[4]

Those on the other side of this Christian debate are called traditionalists, patriarchalists, and considerably less-flattering names.

3. Jürgen Habermas writes helpfully in this regard: "Feminism is . . . directed against a dominant culture that interprets the relationship of the sexes in an asymmetrical manner that excludes equal rights. Gender-specific differences in life circumstances and experiences do not receive adequate consideration, either legally or informally. Women's cultural self-understanding is not given due recognition, any more than their contribution to the common culture; given the prevailing definitions, women's needs cannot even be adequately articulated. Thus, the political struggle for recognition begins as a struggle about the interpretation of gender-specific achievements and interests. Insofar as it is successful, it changes the relationship between the sexes along with the collective identity of women, thereby directly affecting men's self-understanding as well. The scale of values of the society as a whole is up for discussion; the consequences of this problematization extend into core private areas and affect the established boundaries between the private and public spheres as well" (Jürgen Habermas, "Struggles for Recognition in the Democratic Constitutional State," trans. Shierry Weber Nicholsen, in *Multiculturalism*, ed. Amy Gutmann [Princeton: Princeton University Press, 1994], 117).

Luce Irigaray further specifies in this vein that men tend to ignore vast reaches of reality in their typical speaking: "The masculine subject has . . . left behind him nature, woman, and even children." When they do speak, men tend to offer their concepts and proposals as if they were packages and now hand on as objects to another, while women tend to pay more attention to the "transaction" of communication and those involved in it: Masculine speech "must convey a meaning in some way closed, in which the speaking subject converses above all with their own self and with speech. . . . The feminine subject, on the other hand, takes an interest in the relation between two, in communication between people. This subject is thus confronted with a new task as regards the unfolding of speech" (Luce Irigaray, *The Way of Love* [London: Continuum, 2002], 6, 24). Some might retort that all this is simply a contemporary way of expressing the age-old recognition that women and men (tend to) speak and relate differently. Feminism, then, is marked by the affirmation not of the differences but of the equal value of the differences.

4. I am aware of various typologies that feature successive "waves" of feminism and several competing views and agendas among feminists. They include, for example, (1) a "unisex" view that sees men and women as interchangeable parts in society; therefore, feminism means opening every place in society to women; (2) a "complementary" view that sees women and men as essentially different but equally important; therefore, feminism means altering the structures of society in order to profit from distinctly feminine differences; and

The term many of them now prefer is *complementarian*, reflecting their contention that women and men are fully human and reflect the image of God but are sometimes called by God to different and "complementary" roles on the basis of their sex. Furthermore, when social power is in view (as opposed to, say, the power to bear children), then men and women complement each other in that men are to wield it—beneficently, to be sure—and women are to subordinate themselves to it as, indeed, an ordinance of God.

Many have observed that the terms *complementarian* and *egalitarian* can be applied to aspects of each side's viewpoint. Acknowledging that ambiguity, we still need labels, and none better has yet emerged. Therefore, they are used here in what is still the common sense of each.[5]

Most of this book is theological argument. But it really does represent a kind of intellectual and ethical "conversion experi-

---

(3) a "radical" view that sees women as superior to men; therefore, feminism means the advocacy of lesbianism, women-only communities and other social structures, and the like. No detailed maps of these views have won anything approaching universal acceptance in this discourse. And using one or more of these typologies will not advance my purposes in the following discussion, and therefore I need not advocate one or another herein. For helpful introductions to the definition and the history of feminism from a Christian viewpoint, see part 1 of Mary Stewart Van Leeuwen, ed., *After Eden: Facing the Challenge of Gender Reconciliation* (Grand Rapids: Eerdmans, 1993), 19–113; and Elaine Storkey, *Origins of Difference: The Gender Debate Revisited* (Grand Rapids: Baker Academic, 2001).

5. I also recognize, in this terminological morass, that some people resist the term *egalitarian* and similar terms of "equality" because of one or both of the following reservations. First, some worry that "equal" must mean "the same," thus ruling out any sense in which women and men are essentially different. I trust I have made clear that I am not supposing to have answered the age-old question as to whether, and how, women and men differ from each other. *Egalitarian* in this present discussion means "of equal worth, dignity, ability, and calling and therefore not to be discriminated against on the basis of sex where sexual difference cannot be shown to be a relevant factor"—as it is in bearing children, to resort to the obvious example.

Second, some worry that *egalitarian* sounds like it is bound up with the assertion of "rights" in a kind of selfish crusade for the maximization of power for me and my kind. I respond that any leveling of *illegitimate* power and the raising of the downtrodden is entirely biblical. Yes, we human beings—that is to say, we sinners—tend to make trouble whenever we are in power, whether "we" are currently in charge or whether "we" will be in charge tomorrow. Revolutions

ence." So let me begin by opting for the more traditional mode of autobiography—indeed, a sort of "conversion narrative."

My Problem—and the Way Forward

I was raised in a Christian home—indeed, a *really* Christian home: a Plymouth Brethren home, with Brethren roots reaching back for several generations on both sides. Those who know about this small, Protestant denomination know that people in its circles tend to be pretty serious about Christian faith—about Christian doctrine, Christian morality, Christian evangelism, and other good things.

It was not only a Christian home. It was a Focus on the Family-type home. Dad was the full-time breadwinner (a surgeon), and Mom was the full-time homemaker (having quit schoolteaching to bear the first of four children). Dad was an elder in our church and occasionally preached and taught Sunday school, while Mom was an exemplary "Mrs. Elder," helping the church ladies (yes, "ladies": to call them "women" back then would have been impolite) run a myriad of service organizations and charities. She also took her turn playing the piano for worship services.

The Plymouth Brethren have a liturgical tradition that raised the question of gender for me at an early age. Typically, the Brethren celebrate communion at an early service on Sunday mornings, before the main preaching service. The service proceeds with virtually no fixed order of service except perhaps

---

never result in utopias. Still, justice is one of the Bible's constant themes, and the assertion of the rights of women is a cause that Christians have seen and should today continue to see as important. Indeed, the now-global conversation about human rights emerged out of the Christian West. It is the Christian understanding of personhood that grounds this conception. Therefore, the fact that some Christians today are worried, and properly, that some seek to misuse the important principle of human rights for mischievous purposes should not cause us to relinquish this language and this cause. Yes, Christians—and everyone—are to be humble, self-giving, and concerned above all about the glory of God, not our own rights. But let us not settle only for one side of the tension in which God's people live and work. A key part of service to God and the world he loves is the just championing of the rights of all people, particularly the oppressed. So say the prophets, the apostles, and our Lord himself.

for a formal greeting from a presiding elder and a subsequent closing, with the passing of the bread and the cup sometime toward the end of the meeting. During the meeting, anyone can rise and suggest a hymn, which the congregation then sings, or pray aloud, or even offer an exposition of Scripture. Some people prepare well in advance for their participation in the service; others jump up on the spur of an inspiration. The Brethren believe that the Holy Spirit guides the service quite directly, leading first one, then another, to participate—just as 1 Corinthians 14 indicates he will. This free-form openness to the Spirit's leadership amounts to a kind of "charismatic" worship, yet without any tongues-speaking, prophecies, healings, or other spectacular manifestations of the Spirit that would have caused consternation, not celebration, among the Brethren, who are scrupulously opposed to anything "pentecostal."

This kind of meeting—which I often found quite moving—raised the gender question in a fundamental respect. Anyone could lead in this service, not just clergy, for the Brethren are unusual in having no such thing as ordination and therefore no formal clergy. Young people were encouraged to participate as freely as older ones. Anyone, I say, could lead—as long as that one was male.

Thus, I sat in the family pew and observed various men participating week after week. Some did so with evident skill and passion. But others seemed to do so by rote, with little attendant blessing reported by anyone else. I began to wonder why my mother, who was otherwise so esteemed as a leader in our church, remained demurely silent week after week and year after year while Mr. So-and-So rose to bore us once again with his meanderings through Scripture and Mr. Such-and-Such followed with his interminable prayer. When young Bill or even younger Bobby was encouraged to lead in the service while their mothers and grandmothers silently looked on, my wonder deepened.

In my later teens, I began to ask the elders questions about gender. I did so also at the Brethren Bible school I attended and subsequently in the church I attended while at university. I received answers that did not satisfy.

At the same time, I began to encounter more and more Christian women who seemed easily to be the spiritual equals of the men I had seen in church leadership: the sponsor of my high school Christian fellowship, Mrs. Krucker; my aunt Jan, who during the year I boarded with my relatives while at Bible school taught me about the mysteries of women, dating, and marriage in the evenings while my uncle Nelson taught me the New Testament during the days; two other wise and spiritual aunts, Donna-Jean and Valerie, whom I visited whenever I could during my undergraduate years; and the capable InterVarsity Christian Fellowship staff workers I met. I also met women among my fellow students who were obviously at least as mature, at least as wise, at least as gifted, and at least as pious as any of us young men. Radiant among these impressive women was Kari Sleeth, who became my wife, and whose first serious conversation with me was an extended midnight discussion about gender in the church and its apologetical implications. (Yes, it is of such magical moments that true romance is born.)

This was the late 1970s, and therefore all these developments in my life were happening within a broad social transformation of gender. People my age were seeing women enter all occupations, and we were learning to use new, generic titles for them: police officers, firefighters, and flight attendants. There was new talk of a "glass ceiling" that was keeping women from the very top positions in business and the professions, but the fact that it was recognized meant that the glass would shatter soon, as it did in many places. Society at large was making way for women everywhere, if sometimes grudgingly, and increasingly it was scandalous even to grumble about such changes, let alone resist them.

By this point in my life, to echo Thomas Kuhn's helpful terminology in *The Structure of Scientific Revolutions,* the anomalies in my experience were accumulating at a rate too great to be accommodated by my paradigm.[6] And my mental situation was mirrored in my matrimonial one: Kari and I got married after I had completed my first degree, and I left for graduate school with an egalitarian marriage but without a thoroughly constructed theological basis for it. Finally, one afternoon, while studying in the tiny living room

---

6. Thomas S. Kuhn, *The Structure of Scientific Revolutions,* 2nd ed. (1962; repr., Chicago: University of Chicago Press, 1970).

of our student apartment in Chicago while Kari was at work at the hospital across the street, I underwent an explosive paradigm shift. Yes, we come at last to the promised key to the lock, the clue to the puzzle, the Answer to the Problem.

I had been struggling with gender questions again and had been reading about various sides of the issue. At the crucial moment I have described, I had been reading yet another explanation of 1 Timothy 2:11–15, easily one of the most obscure of the classic passages on this matter. I remember quite clearly now—more than twenty years later—putting the book down on my lap and realizing this insight: Nobody could explain this passage.

To be sure, I had been reading more than a dozen *attempts* to explain this passage. Some of them were ingenious; a few were even likely. But it struck me with paradigm-shaking force that no one could explain all the clauses in this passage with full plausibility. I then began to think that this problem was true not only of expositions of this one text but of the whole gender question. No one I had read (and I had read quite a few) could put all the relevant texts together into a single, finished puzzle with no pieces left over, with none manufactured to fill in gaps, and with none forced into place. I began to recall, with mounting excitement, how champions of one view typically ignored or explained away the leading texts of champions of other views. (This phenomenon is what lawyers call avoiding or finessing the "bad facts" of a case.)

I came to a principle of general theological method out of this wrestling with a particular issue, that of gender: We should not wait to come to a theological conclusion until the happy day in which we have perfectly arranged all the relevant texts. Instead, we should look at all the texts as open-mindedly as possible and see if among the various competing interpretations there is one that makes the most sense of the most texts and especially the most important ones. We should look, in basic epistemological terms, for the preponderance of warrants or grounds to believe p instead of q. If no such preponderance is evident, then we should suspend making a decision. But if we do conclude that a preponderance is discernible, then we should acknowledge it—indeed, be grateful for it—and proceed to act on that basis. For what else can we do in theology?

Jaroslav Pelikan, among many other historians of doctrine, has shown how the New Testament provides texts about the nature of the incarnation that can fairly be read as supporting various heresies (such as adoptionism, Arianism, modalism, and Nestorianism), while the church has concluded that the *best* reading of the *most* texts, including the *most important* texts, leads to the conclusions of the Chalcedonian definition of 451.[7] Predestination and free will, faith and works, so-called charismatic phenomena, the nature of the end times—who can seriously suggest that there is one and only one theological position on such controversies that provides the best interpretation of every single relevant text and packages them together in an effortlessly coherent whole? (Christians have done exactly that for centuries, of course. I just think they have been wrong to do so.)

So, I concluded, the theological task is not to be understood as "figuring it all out" so that one day a person or a church can finally say, "There, now! That's the answer!" with precision and certainty. The task instead is to dwell on the Bible, with the help of the Holy Spirit and the church; to make the best decision one can make about what Scripture means; and then to respond to it in faith, obedience, and gratitude. Indeed, such a posture of interpretative humility entails remaining continually open to refinement of one's interpretations and even to the acceptance of quite different positions as the Holy Spirit gives one more light. (I hope you will maintain that posture as you read, just in case the Holy Spirit offers something new to you as you do so.)

I went on to recognize that champions of various positions sometimes attacked one another's views—and often one another—on grounds that were not theological. Feminists accused traditionalists of sexism: Traditionalists claimed to believe that women and men are equal but then relegated women to subservient positions in church and home—and society too, in the case of telling women to stay home and look after their husbands and children. Traditionalists could never explain why it was

---

7. Jaroslav Pelikan, *The Emergence of the Catholic Tradition (100–600)*, vol. 1, *The Christian Tradition* (Chicago: University of Chicago Press, 1971), 175–210.

better for all women everywhere to remain in these domestic roles while all men everywhere were to be breadwinners out in the marketplace. Wasn't this scheme simply a baptized version of modern social sector differentiation, a phenomenon that emerged only in postagrarian industrial societies? This domestic arrangement was not in fact *traditional* at all—except in the historically shortsighted sense of "what Mom and Dad did back in the 1950s and 1960s." So why should such roles be acclaimed as perennially normative?[8]

Furthermore, feminists argued, there did not seem to be anything essential to being a woman that made her unfit for leadership in home, church, or society, and traditionalists rarely suggested (anymore) that there was an inherent flaw of this sort. In the bad old days, women were derided as emotional, irrational, illogical, defensive, and the like and therefore truly seemed unfit for important responsibilities.[9] (One can still, alas, make a lot of money telling people that "men are from Mars and women are from Venus.")[10] Thus, women were instead put

8. "Even in simple subsistence societies there are almost no activities that are universally the domain of only women or men. The few exceptions center around childbearing and nursing activities, which are biologically restricted to women, and activities such as making war, acquiring raw materials, and dealing with large animals, most of which require male strength. What is universal is the higher status of whatever is considered 'men's work.' If in one culture it is men who build houses and women who make baskets, then that culture will see house building as more important than basket weaving. In another culture, perhaps right next door, where women construct houses and men make baskets, basket weaving will have higher social status than house building. (This example comes from my own field work in West Africa.) In fact, such differences may even become a basis for cultural chauvinism: 'they' cannot possibly be normal human beings like 'us,' because their men do women's work, and they let their women do men's work!" (Mary Stewart Van Leeuwen, *Gender and Grace: Love, Work, and Parenting in a Changing World* [Downers Grove, IL: InterVarsity, 1990], 113–14; cf. Bernard T. Adeney, *Strange Virtues: Ethics in a Multicultural World* [Downers Grove, IL: InterVarsity, 1995], chap. 9, for a useful discussion also in international context).

9. It must be acknowledged that the writings of eminent ancient theologians are littered with disparaging, even misogynistic, references to women of exactly this sort. In brief compass, Elaine Storkey quotes Tertullian, Clement of Alexandria, Jerome, and Thomas Aquinas (*Origins of Difference*, 98).

10. John Gray, *Men Are from Mars, Women Are from Venus* (New York: Harper, 1994).

in charge of children (!) and given other domestic jobs that, for men in the marketplace and in church leadership, were relatively uninteresting and unimportant. And that all made a kind of sense: If women couldn't handle leadership, then it was best that they weren't given any.[11]

Rarely, however, does one hear that sort of argument today. Instead, traditionalists tend to fall over themselves praising women to the skies as fully equal to men. It is not that women are inferior, they say; it is just that God wants women not to lead in home and church (and possibly elsewhere), and we should not disobey God. What has not been made clear in the current debate, feminists maintain, is just *why* God would want that when he seems—by all accounts, on every side of this issue—to have made women evidently quite capable of leadership in all other spheres of society.[12] (Margaret Thatcher's career as British prime minister in the 1970s and 1980s loomed large as a case in point throughout the English-speaking world. Women as chief executives in businesses, universities, hospitals, and other institutions have multiplied the local and national examples.)

---

11. We encounter herein a deep irony, accentuated during the "cult of true womanhood" in the nineteenth century. Women simultaneously are told that they are not capable of leadership—by which is meant certain kinds of public leadership, such as business and politics—but also that they are extremely important in shaping the entire next generation, as in the saying that "the hand that rocks the cradle rules the world." One also might ask the question, If women are not capable of thinking straight, why put them in charge of teaching impressionable children, the audience least capable of detecting their errors and compensating for their shortcomings?

12. Jonathan Edwards, hero of many evangelicals, was himself perplexed on this very point: "Many women in Christian churches are much more capable than some of the men." He went on, "It will be found difficult to say what there is in nature that shows that a wise woman ought not to have as much power in the church as a male servant that hasn't a tenth part of the understanding." Edwards reserved church leadership for men only, despite his obvious regard for women in general and for a number of particular women in his own life whom he saw as spiritual heroes (not least his own wife, Sarah), because he thought the Bible told him to do so. (For these citations, see George M. Marsden, *Jonathan Edwards: A Life* [New Haven: Yale University Press, 2003], 346. Marsden notes that Edwards did allow Sarah to exhort mixed adult audiences in the full flower of the Awakening, since she could testify to an extraordinary experience for the edification of all [244].)

God seems to have good reasons for his other commands. What is his good reason for this one?[13]

Among the most powerful arguments offered in turn by complementarians was the charge of arrogance: Why did feminists imply, if they did not say outright, that the rest of the Christian church since the time of the apostles was wrong in regard to gender? Given the virtually unbroken tradition of patriarchy—male leadership and authority—with exceptions too few and too eccentric (if not heretical and schismatic) to take seriously, how dare egalitarians suggest that they alone, and only today, teach the truth about the correct relations of men and women? Indeed, most of the contemporary global church continues to organize itself in terms of male leadership. Egalitarians, therefore, are implicitly claiming that those Christians also are either mistaken on a basic point of Christian practice or are instead willfully perpetuating sinful structures of male domination and female oppression. In short, many complementarians say, egalitarians claim that everyone else has been either too stupid or too sinful to see the light.

These sorts of extrabiblical accusations remind us that Christians make decisions not only on the basis of Bible study but also as we consult tradition, reason, and experience—the four elements of the so-called Wesleyan Quadrilateral. (To these resources the Roman Catholic Church adds the authoritative teaching office of the church, personified in the pope.) And we properly consult these resources not on our own but in the

13. This book is written partly in response to the dilemma many contemporary Christians feel: God seems to have instituted patriarchy, but patriarchy itself seems unfair and unhelpful, particularly as it has given license to abuse through the centuries. I have in mind such well-meaning people as Stephen Carter, who, after remarking on the propensity of men to take advantage of their wives under the aegis of Christian "headship," concludes, "God, for reasons no human will know, inspired Paul to appoint the husband as the head of the wife. But in our mortal fallibility, humans, mainly men, constructed a world in which the exercise of that office is often unjust. For that we should blame men, not God—not women, and certainly not feminism, which has been but the bearer of the tidings and has, in that way, played a role in the fulfillment of God's mysterious purpose" (Stephen L. Carter, *Integrity* [New York: Basic Books, 1996], 151). We can reduce the mystery here and make much more sense of what Paul, and God, are doing in Scripture and in the church.

company of the church—the church of the past and the church of the present—seeking guidance from the Holy Spirit through these resources. Theology is the task of coordinating the deliverances of these gifts of God and then formulating our best estimation of what God is saying to us today, in this context, for his purposes.

It is deficient theology, therefore, that halts all deliberation with mere proof-texting ("The Bible says it; I believe it; that settles it"); or with appeals to current social practice ("Women lead businesses, universities, and governments—it is just ridiculous not to have them lead churches"); or with claims of personal intuition ("I just feel led to pastoral leadership"); or with any other shortcut. Furthermore, it is disturbing how many churchgoers are content to settle for such simplistic methods, which are so clearly vulnerable to manipulation by one's own or others' interests.

Likewise, many Christians affirm that only arrogant theology suggests that this or that formulation of doctrine or practice is a perfectly formulated and timeless truth for the ages. We revere the great creeds; we honor the great catechisms and confessions; we receive the liturgical, political, devotional, and other traditions of our forebears with respect and gratitude. But we are careful not to confuse those treasures with the gospel itself, or with the supremely authoritative Bible, or with the ongoing guidance of the Holy Spirit of God in the current life of this part of the church. We are open to hearing fresh words of God that help this part of the church cooperate with God in the work of his kingdom in its particular situation.

Two More Principles

Let's consider just two more methodological points that helped me move beyond my tense position of wanting to be a feminist but not seeing how I could justify such a move given the biblical texts that seemed to forbid it.

The first principle deals with "control texts." While all the Bible is inspired by God, there are texts of the Bible that clearly dominate our interpretation and reception of the others. Most obvious is Jesus' own summary of the law in the two great commandments to love God with all one has and is and to love one's neighbor as oneself. On these two commands, Jesus says, "hang all the law and the prophets" (Matt. 22:40). Theologians recognize, then, that some texts are more fundamental than others in any given discussion. But deciding which texts occupy which place on a hierarchy of "control texts" is not always easy.

In this debate, egalitarians tend to use Galatians 3:28 as a text that governs everything else: "There is no longer Jew or Greek, there is no longer slave or free, there is no longer male and female; for all of you are one in Christ Jesus." Complementarians reply that this text should be more narrowly understood as applying to salvation, not to every aspect of life here and now. They point out, for example, that the difference between Jews and Greeks was acknowledged in the great council of Acts 15 and that the system of slavery was condoned by Paul in numerous writings in which he addresses slaves and masters (notably in the Epistle to Philemon but also in parallel passages dealing with household relations in Eph. 6 and Col. 3; cf. 1 Pet. 2). So it does not make sense to assume that Galatians 3:28 means that no Christian distinction should properly remain between male and female.

For their part, many complementarians argue that, whatever else may be ambiguous or controversial in the Bible about gender, it is clear that women are to "remain silent" in church meetings: "As in all the churches of the saints, women should be silent in the churches. For they are not permitted to speak, but should be subordinate, as the law also says. If there is anything they desire to know, let them ask their husbands at home. For it is shameful for a woman to speak in church" (1 Cor. 14:33–35; cf. 1 Tim. 2:11–12).

Egalitarians respond that this understanding of Paul's instructions seems a curious one given that earlier in the same epistle he gave instructions for women to cover their heads precisely when they "pray or prophesy." One might argue that the praying in view here is merely private prayer, although it seems unlikely given that the theme of this section is corporate, not individual, worship. Furthermore, prophecy intrinsically is a corporate activity. One hardly prophesies to oneself, no matter the context! Therefore, egalitarians argue, Paul *cannot* have enjoined "silence" as the total absence of women's voices in public services.

Thus, we recognize both the importance and the peril of discerning which texts are most fundamental, which texts properly "control" the interpretation of other texts, as we work at theology. Indeed, we recognize the importance of the so-called hermeneutical circle here: the moving back and forth between what one assumes are control texts and what one assumes are secondary texts, seeing how well the data are explained by this relationship, with the possibility ever open that one not only might have to adjust one's interpretation of this or that text but also might have to move texts from one category to another as one works toward the best arrangement of them all.

The hermeneutical circle—or, as some hopefully put it, the hermeneutical *spiral* that gets us closer and closer to the truth—shows up also in the last consideration in this chapter. When we investigate a matter, we are always moving back and forth between our general idea of what is going on and the particular bits of information we have gathered from which we interpret what is going on. Indeed, as we gather new bits, or reinterpret bits we already have on hand, we confirm the general idea, adjust it, or even replace it with a different general idea. Yet we also recognize that we always have a general idea of some sort that is governing our interpretation of the bits. If we did not have a general idea of this sort, we would not know even what sorts of bits to look for, what questions to ask of them, or what categories in which to place them. Thus, we experience a dialectic, a back-and-forth motion between the parts and the whole.

One of the important implications of this view of how we think about things is that we can, so to speak, enter the circle/spiral anywhere we like, at either the level of the general or at the level of the particular. In the latter case, that of entering at the level of the particular, many Christians believe that the best way to proceed theologically is to gather all the relevant bits together—from tradition, reason, experience, and especially the

Bible—and then try to discern what general pattern best explains them all. This, in a simplified form, is *induction*. But this way of thinking fails to acknowledge what we have just recognized: that we always have a general pattern in mind that sets up and guides the investigation in the first place. For example, we always assume certain criteria of relevance for selecting the relevant bits. We are never just looking at the data. Still, we can proceed in this way, although now more properly self-conscious of the role being played by our preconceptions as we gather data. Aware of our biases, we can try to be not too prejudiced as we induce a general theory from our investigation.

We can proceed a different way, however—at the level of the general theory or hypothesis. We can acknowledge that we have preconceptions. If we have devised a fairly elaborate theory, then the properly critical thing to do is to articulate this theory—a generalization based on previous encounters with relevant data— and then test it, particularly against not only all the data we can find but also all the data and all the countervailing arguments offered by opponents of the theory. If the theory stands up well against these tests, then we can enjoy reasonable confidence in it.

But let's consider other possible outcomes. If our theory fails to explain some data as well as a competing theory does, we still are justified in maintaining allegiance to our theory if the competing theory does not, overall, do a better job of explaining all the relevant data and responding to all counterarguments. The quest is not for the *perfect* theory, the *perfect* interpretation of Scripture, the *perfect* theology but for the best available. The main thing in life is not to figure everything out but to rely on God to provide what we need to accomplish his will in every circumstance—including the best theology for the job—and then to get on with that work.

To be sure, if our theory does not do a noticeably better job than at least one other counter-theory, then perhaps the best conclusion is a suspension of allegiance to *any* theory, pending more data or better arguments. But real life often compels us to act before we have an opinion that is clearly superior to all others, in which case we are still justified in holding to our previous theory—but with considerable humility and with readiness to have it improved or replaced as the occasion arises.

With this consideration in view, then, here is how I would like to proceed. I was taught to think the inductive way as a Christian. In this case, that would mean working through Bible texts one by one, then going on to the history of theology and of the church's gender practices, and finally trying to sort all this out in light of contemporary gender studies and social experiences. But I think it worthwhile—and perhaps more efficient for the purpose of this book—to try something else. The next chapter sets out a theory, a model for understanding gender. It is a model based on fundamental Christian considerations, such as the nature of the church, the mission of God in the world, the characteristic way the Holy Spirit fulfills that mission, and so on. Along the way, I explain some of the implications of this theory for the Christian home and church, as well as for society at large. I also offer arguments supporting this theory from the Bible, the history of the church, and contemporary reason and experience. Finally, I test this theory by posing against it the objections of counter-theories.

Am I a completely objective adjudicator of these various competing theories and thus capable of rendering an infallible and universally valid judgment? Of course not. But then, neither are you! We cannot escape our limitations and imperfections. Nor can we evade, or even indefinitely defer, our responsibility to make up our mind and live as obediently as we can in the light of what we perceive to be God's Word. So let me introduce the understanding of gender that replaced my traditional one, and let's see how well it works.

2

The Paradigm

As one reads the recent Christian literature on gender, it is impressive how confident, even univocal, are so many authors. No one quite says this, but the implication is clear: "My position is simply the right position, and all who differ are simply wrong. They are badly confused—if not *evil* in willfully resisting the patent truth of what I'm saying."

Let me say immediately that there are some Christian affirmations that are basic and clear. Christianity is properly univocal in its condemnation of pride, lust, greed, and the other deadly sins. One must say, "Jesus is Lord," or one is not a Christian in any spiritually important sense. Much in the Bible is not just true (which I believe all of the Bible to be) but simply and clearly true.

Yet it is evident that the Bible offers more complicated wisdom on certain matters. In some cases, what was once allowed is now condemned: for example, divorce by a simple writ by a dissatisfied husband (Matt. 5:31–32). In some cases, what was once commanded is now done away with as otiose: for example, the entire Old Testament sacrificial system, as interpreted in the Epistle to the Hebrews. In some cases, what is mandated for some is not mandated for others: for example, adherence to the Jewish law by Jewish Christians but not by Gentile Christians (Acts 15:23–29). In some cases, what is troubling to some is declared to be of no consequence, *unless* such a thing would trouble one's conscience or cause another Christian confusedly to stumble back into sinful ways, in which case it is indeed important: The same example paradoxically serves for both principles, namely, eating meat offered to idols (1 Cor. 8; cf. 10:25–30; Rom. 14:14–23). Yes, the Bible's teaching is often complex, subtle, and even ambiguous—for the trained interpreter as well as for the lay reader.

That was not, however, what I wanted to conclude when I thought about gender. I wanted to think simply and clearly about it. In particular, I wanted to be a feminist all the way. I wanted to see women and men as coequal partners before God, bearers together of God's image, with no job or role or responsibility closed to either of them except where sheer biology dictated. This simple position made the most sense of the world around me, made the most sense of my experiences with capable women both within and outside the church, and made the most sense of my relationship with my wife. But it did not make the most sense of the tradition of the church, nor did it square with a number of Bible verses that seemed forthrightly to forbid a woman from exercising coequal leadership in family or congregation.

Now, let me pause to recognize that I run the risk in what follows of oversimplifying the situation. There are not simply two positions on gender among evangelicals but several. For example, some evangelicals allow women to preach but only in foreign missionary situations (what I call "the missionary exception"). Others allow women to participate in spiritual leadership but only in so-called parachurch organizations, not in congregations and denominations (what I call "the parachurch parenthesis"). Still others permit women to have wide-ranging theological careers of speaking and writing as long as they profess to be responsible to a man, whether husband or pastor or both (the "under authority arrangement"). I, however, did not want to rest in any of these intermediate models but sought a full-blown egalitarianism. Those are the terms of the following discussion as well.[1]

I propose, then, a paradigm of gender that does, indeed, draw no lines between men and women as to role in home, church, or society—beyond those required by biology. Unlike many egalitarians, however, I qualify this radical position. I do so in some ways so drastic that many egalitarians will reject it. In fact, some likely will doubt my commitment to feminism. Yet this paradigm to me makes the most sense of most of the most important data and a number of smaller details as well. So I will hold to it—unless a better paradigm comes into view.

Equality

The first principle of this paradigm is that men and women are equal in every way. Genesis 1 records that the human being was created in God's image and as male and female in that image (Gen. 1:26–27). The "creation mandate" to procreate and to co-create the world with God is given to man and woman as the partners they are—the humans—without gender differentiation.

The second, and different, creation story of Genesis 2 shows the human being divided by God into male and female. The self-consciousness of the previously undivided human "goes with" the male, and it is he who then recognizes and celebrates the female as his partner upon their differentiation. But the passage continues into a celebration of marriage: Two human beings join together as they separate from their birth families, literally re-forming the originally undivided human (Gen. 2:18–24). I cannot imagine a stronger set of images of coequality, partnership, and the like.

1. For indications of evangelical pluralism on these issues, when most commentators reduce the conversation to just two options, see Jack Buckley, "Paul, Women, and the Church: How Fifteen Modern Interpreters Understand Five Key Passages," *Eternity* 31 (December 1980): 30–35; and John G. Stackhouse, Jr., "Women in Public Ministry: Five Models in North American Evangelicalism," in *Evangelical Landscapes: Facing Critical Issues of the Day* (Grand Rapids: Baker Academic, 2002), 121–39.

As we pass over, for now, the fall in Genesis 3 and the subsequent history of redemption, we encounter Jesus befriending and teaching women—sometimes to the scandal of onlookers, given the strict separation of the sexes in public—and women caring for him in return. Among numerous examples, the most prominent perhaps are the Samaritan woman (John 4), Mary Magdalene (Mark 15:40–41; Luke 8:1–3), and Mary and Martha (Luke 10:38–42; John 11:1–44; 12:1–8). Jesus repeatedly "trespasses" across the gender lines of his culture to affirm, serve, and enjoy women as he also delights in men.

We next encounter the Holy Spirit being poured out on women and men together as the prophecy of Joel is invoked to explain the spectacle of Pentecost (Acts 2:16–18). We encounter Galatians 3:28 and the declaration that in Christ all the barriers that divide people from one another into better and worse, insiders and outsiders, are done away: no more first-class versus second-class citizens in the kingdom of Christ; no Jew feeling more holy than the mere Gentile; no male lording it over the female; no free person exploiting the slave. We encounter lists of spiritual gifts and church functions that are never categorized as "for men only," "for women only," and "for both" (e.g., Rom. 12:6–8; 1 Cor. 12:8–10, 27–30; Eph. 4:11). We also encounter Paul sending commendatory words about women playing various roles in the churches to which he writes—including women identified as coworker, deacon, and even apostle (Rom. 16:1–12).

Many scriptural clues, therefore, indicate that egalitarians are right: God originally intended women and men to be co-equal partners in stewarding the earth, without role differentiation, and he has never rescinded that mandate. Indeed, in God's renewal of all things, in his great salvation plan to restore shalom, men and women will treat each other as they were intended to treat each other. We already see this renewed order in the inbreaking of the kingdom evident in the New Testament.

Yet egalitarians often fail to listen to their complementarian brothers and sisters who point out several cogent objections, or at least qualifications, to this vision. First, the testimony of most of the Bible—from Genesis 3 until the last epistles of the New Testament—bespeaks a pattern of patriarchy. Men are in charge, and they are supposed to be in charge.

Second, God depicts his own relationship with Israel, and then Christ's with the church, in terms of a patriarchal marriage of non-equals. God/Christ is the superior power, the initiator and sustainer of the relationship, the leader and the provider, while Israel/church is the grateful respondent.[2]

Third, Jesus does indeed welcome women into his circle of disciples—but not his inner circle. That is reserved for the Twelve, not one of whom is a woman. Many scholars argue that the Twelve are symbolic of the new Israel Jesus is constituting in his ministry. Why, then, does he select twelve free Jewish males? Why not Jewish women? Or Gentiles? Or slaves? Why so much symbolic continuity with the distinctions of class, ethnicity, and sex typical of the old covenant if the new Israel is to do away with all such distinctions? To be sure, the Twelve are a first-generation class that gives way after their deaths to elders, teachers, prophets, and other leaders—some of whom, egalitarians rush to point out, seem to have been women. But the point remains that Jesus "transgresses" only so far in his public life—to the point of occasional scandal but not of gender revolution.

For his part, Paul recognizes and affirms women's service to the church. But he also expressly forbids (at least some) women to teach or to have authority over (at least some) men (at least sometimes). Indeed, women apparently are to keep silent in church services (1 Cor. 14:33–35; cf. 1 Tim. 2:11–12). Therefore, whatever else women do—and complementarians insist that women are invaluable members of churches then and now—Paul seems to teach that they are not to lead.

I would like to suggest a way to understand gender that pays respect to both sides, a way that avoids simply ruling out the contentions of either side, since I find valid points in each, and, perhaps more significantly, since exemplary Christians advocate both positions. (Again, the only alternative is to con-

2. See appendix B for further discussion of this point.

clude that all those holy and intelligent people who disagree with me are just plain wrong—and that seems unlikely in the extreme.) In particular, I would like to find a way to keep from suggesting that the Bible contradicts itself and to avoid the intolerable conclusion that Jesus and Paul contradict themselves.[3] To do so, I need to outline a set of principles that, taken together, both justify and qualify Christian egalitarianism in home, church, and society.

Gospel Priorities and Holy Pragmatism

If equality is the first principle in this paradigm, the second principle is that some things matter more than others. Thus, some things are to be sacrificed in the interest of the greater good. In particular, what matters most is the furtherance of the gospel message. In the New Testament, and in subsequent church history, we see that God is willing to do almost anything to get the gospel to as many people as possible, as effectively as possible. He then wants this message to take root and to bear as

3. Among evangelicals of a previous generation, Paul Jewett's pronouncement came as a shock: "There is no satisfying way to harmonize the Pauline argument for female subordination with the larger Christian vision of which the great apostle to the Gentiles was himself the primary architect" (Paul K. Jewett, *Man as Male and Female: A Study of Sexual Relationships from a Theological Point of View* [Grand Rapids: Eerdmans, 1975], 112–13]. I hope the model I present will be found to be a satisfactory harmonization.

I have no patience with the common casting of Paul as the villain and Jesus as the hero in the drama of feminism in the New Testament. For one thing, Jesus and Paul have similar, not different, teachings and practices regarding gender, as I show in this chapter. For another, there *is* no "Jesus" in the New Testament except as mediated by other authors, since Jesus did not write any of the canon himself. In the New Testament, therefore, we have the Evangelists' versions of Jesus, but we also have Paul's, Peter's, and others'—albeit in epistolary rather than gospel form. There is no compelling reason to privilege Matthew's or Luke's version of Jesus above Peter's or Paul's. Finally, orthodox teaching about inspiration declares that Jesus is, in a fundamental respect, the Author of *all* the New Testament, as it is the Spirit of God who superintends the production of Holy Scripture. Pitting "Jesus" against "Paul," therefore, is both a literary and a theological mistake and should be relegated to the dustbin of nineteenth-century German scholarship from whence it arose.

much fruit as possible. We see also that God expects his people to participate in what we might call this holy pragmatism.[4]

God is willing to forgo the achievement of secondary objectives in the interest of furthering his primary purposes, and he expects us to do the same. We may wonder why God Almighty does not just accomplish all his purposes entirely and at once. But we are now asking the age-old question of the nature of God's providence, within which lie such profound matters as the so-called delay of the parousia, the problem of evil, and so on. Clearly, we cannot set out a full-blown doctrine of providence here, but we must bear in mind the truth that God's providence has a different timetable than we may prefer. His ways are higher than our ways, his thoughts higher than our thoughts (Isa. 55:9).

Among those ways and thoughts of God, then, is the principle of accommodation. God works within human limitations—both individual and corporate—to transform the world according to his good purposes. To be blunt, God works with what he's got and with what we've got. He does not create a whole new situation but instead graciously pursues shalom in the glory and the mess we have made. The living water of the Holy Spirit pours over the extant topography of the social landscape and rarely sweeps all before it. The Spirit usually conforms himself to the contours he encounters. But as he does so, like an irresistible flow of water, he reshapes them by and by, eventually making the crooked ways straight and the rough places a plain (Isa. 40:3–4).[5]

William Webb offers a helpful summary of reasons God may have acted in a gradual, accommodating way regarding patriarchy:

> *Pastoral*: to "stretch" the covenant people as far as they could go (like an elastic band), but not wanting them to "snap." Change is always difficult. God brings his people along in ways that were

---

4. I do not mean "pragmatism" in the technical epistemological sense but in the colloquial sense of "practicality," of "focusing on getting the job done."

5. This insight is typical of David Martin, who uses slightly different images to the same effect: "The lava of the Spirit runs along the lines of social fault; and the wind of the Spirit blows according to a chart of high and low pressures" (*Reflections on Sociology and Theology* [Oxford: Clarendon, 1997], 67).

feasible adaptations. *Pedagogical*: to take people from where they are (the known) and help them move to a foreseeable future (the unknown) that has enough continuity with the present so that they can find their way into the preferred future. *Evangelistic*: to make the Christian lifestyle evangelistically winsome to unbelievers. The reform was enough to better existing sociological structures, but not so radical that it would jeopardize other aspects of Christian mission or overtly threaten governmental structures. *Competing values*: to sustain other good values at least temporarily within a less redemptive framework. . . . *Soteriological*: to deal with humanity's sinful and stubborn condition. Reform does not come easily to a dark side within fallen humanity. God's revelation took measured steps (not unrealistic leaps) in the progressive sanctification of social structures.[6]

In the same pattern of divine behavior, therefore, we encounter the apparent scandal of Jesus not healing everyone, or delivering everyone from captivity, or raising everyone from the dead. In response, Christians believe in God's providence and therefore that it was more strategic for Jesus to limit his array of miracles—primarily to be signs of the inbreaking of the kingdom through him and thus signs of his authority and identity. We trust that God's self-limitation is somehow for the greater good of his ultimate purposes.[7]

In just the same way, Jesus presses against the gender expectations of his culture—the way he also does against the Jew/Gentile distinction, the Jew/Samaritan distinction, the adult/child distinction, the rich/poor distinction, and so on—but without actually overturning them. Jesus treats patriarchy the way he treats much else of the law and custom of his time: ambiguously, suggestively, and sometimes subversively but never immediately revolutionarily outside the central matter of his own mission and person. (Thus, I am disagreeing with my feminist friends who think we can read egalitarianism directly out of the career of Jesus.) Jesus puts first things first: the gospel of the kingdom of God brought near in

---

6. William J. Webb, *Slaves, Women, and Homosexuals* (Downers Grove, IL: InterVarsity, 2001), 255.

7. I explore some of these issues further in *Can God Be Trusted? Faith and the Challenge of Evil* (New York: Oxford University Press, 1998).

himself. The main scandal of Jesus' career is properly *Jesus*—not Jesus and feminism, or Jesus and the abolition of slavery, or Jesus and Jewish emancipation, or Jesus and anything else. Those other causes are good, and they are implicit in Jesus' ministry. But they are incipient at best, and Jesus' accommodation to these various social distinctions needs to be acknowledged and then accounted for in one's paradigm regarding gender.

Recall again, then, this central pattern of God's activity: God gives all he has and does all he can do within the situation he has sovereignly allowed to develop. He constantly sacrifices good things for better. Indeed, he "did not withhold his own Son" (Rom. 8:32) but gave his life in order to secure the greater good of global redemption. He expects us to "make up the sufferings of Christ": to work, to suffer, and even to die alongside him—indeed, to take up our crosses in daily acknowledgment that we are both his children and his slaves, as the apostles designate themselves (Col. 1:24).

We would not need to concern ourselves with this matter of gospel priorities if the kingdom had indeed fully come two thousand years ago. We will not need to rank them in the New Jerusalem, for shalom will have blossomed forth on every hand. As Christ showed Julian of Norwich, "All will be well, and all will be well, and all manner of thing will be well."[8]

You and I live now, however, in "the meanwhile." It is a commonplace of New Testament scholarship regarding the kingdom of God that it has come "already but not yet": God's direct and glorious rule is already and authentically here, through Jesus Christ, but it is not yet fully realized in this world still marred by sin. So we encounter a third principle, one not always accounted for properly in discussions of gender: eschatology.

Eschatology

Egalitarians often accuse complementarians of failing to recognize the inbreaking of the kingdom of God and thus failing to

8. Julian of Norwich, *Revelations of Divine Love*, trans. Clifton Wolters (Harmondsworth, UK: Penguin, 1966), 103 (chap. 27).

take eschatology seriously—particularly the prospect that the last days have come. "You are living in the past," egalitarians say, "still living under the effects of the fall and thus perpetuating the male domination described in Genesis 3. You do not realize that we are in a new era, the era of the last days, when patriarchy, along with other traditional compromises of God's good will, is to be done away."

Yet egalitarians are open to an opposite charge, namely, that they are practicing a "realized eschatology"—some would say an "over-realized eschatology"—that is, an eschatology that acts as if the end times have indeed fully come and that we are to experience all the blessings of the kingdom already. If there is too little "already" in the complementarian position, there is not enough "not yet" in most egalitarian teaching.

What, however, would our understanding of gender look like if we took the "already but not yet" principle seriously? What if we were to expect, instead of one extreme or the other, an appropriately paradoxical situation: a slow and partial realization of gospel values here and there, as God patiently and carefully works his mysterious ways along the multiple fronts of kingdom advance?

Priorities, Pragmatism, and Eschatology

The New Testament writers and audiences seem to expect the Lord's return at any time—and certainly within the lifetime of some of the first readers. Indeed, Paul has to counsel the Thessalonians that the Lord has not returned already but is expected soon (1 Thess. 4:13–5:3). So it would make sense—given gospel priorities, holy pragmatism, and eschatological expectations—for the apostles to teach a policy of social conservatism ("Get along as best you can with the political powers and social structures that be") in the interest of spreading the gospel as far and as fast as possible. And they do.[9]

9. John Howard Yoder says, "The concern of the Apostle is . . . to assist everyone to remain 'free from anxieties' [1 Cor. 7:32] in a world whose structures are impermanent, and not so important that we should concentrate our efforts

This outlook is so foreign to most modern Christians—although many Pentecostals and charismatics around the world share such a lively belief in the imminence of the second coming—that it is worth considering several key passages in this regard, three from Paul and one from Peter:

> But we urge you, beloved, . . . to aspire to live quietly, to mind your own affairs, and to work with your hands, as we directed you, so that you may behave properly toward outsiders and be dependent on no one.
>
> 1 Thessalonians 4:10–12

> If it is possible, so far as it depends on you, live peaceably with all. Beloved, never avenge yourselves, but leave room for the wrath of God; for it is written, "Vengeance is mine, I will repay, says the Lord." No, "if your enemies are hungry, feed them; if they are thirsty, give them something to drink; for by doing this you will heap burning coals on their heads." Do not be overcome by evil, but overcome evil with good.
>
> Let every person be subject to the governing authorities; for there is no authority except from God, and those authorities that exist have been instituted by God. Therefore whoever resists authority resists what God has appointed, and those who resist will incur judgment. For rulers are not a terror to good conduct, but to bad. Do you wish to have no fear of the authority? Then do what is good, and you will receive its approval; for it is God's servant for your good. But if you do what is wrong, you should be afraid, for the authority does not bear the sword in vain! It is the servant of God to execute wrath on the wrongdoer. Therefore one must be subject, not only because of wrath but also because of conscience. For the same reason you also pay taxes, for the authorities are God's servants, busy with this very thing. Pay to

---

upon changing our status with regard to them. . . . Thus the Christian is called to view his social status from the perspective of maximizing his freedom. If an opportunity is given him to exercise more freedom, he shall do so because it is to freedom that we are called in Christ. But that freedom can already be realized within his present status by voluntarily accepting subordination, in view of the relative unimportance of such social distinctions when seen in the light of the coming fulfillment of God's purposes" (*The Politics of Jesus* [Grand Rapids: Eerdmans, 1972], 186–87).

all what is due them—taxes to whom taxes are due, revenue to whom revenue is due, respect to whom respect is due, honor to whom honor is due.

Owe no one anything, except to love one another; for the one who loves another has fulfilled the law. The commandments, "You shall not commit adultery; You shall not murder; You shall not steal; You shall not covet"; and any other commandment, are summed up in this word, "Love your neighbor as yourself." Love does no wrong to a neighbor; therefore, love is the fulfilling of the law.

Besides this, you know what time it is, how it is now the moment for you to wake from sleep. For salvation is nearer to us now than when we became believers; the night is far gone, the day is near.

Romans 12:18–13:12

Let each of you remain in the condition in which you were called.

Were you a slave when called? Do not be concerned about it. Even if you can gain your freedom, make use of your present condition now more than ever. For whoever was called in the Lord as a slave is a freed person belonging to the Lord, just as whoever was free when called is a slave of Christ. You were bought with a price; do not become slaves of human masters. In whatever condition you were called, brothers and sisters, there remain with God. . . . For the present form of this world is passing away.

1 Corinthians 7:20–24, 31; cf. 1 Timothy 6:1; Titus 2:9–10[10]

Conduct yourselves honorably among the Gentiles, so that, though they malign you as evildoers, they may see your honorable deeds and glorify God when he comes to judge.

For the Lord's sake accept the authority of every human institution, whether of the emperor as supreme, or of governors, as sent by him to punish those who do wrong and to praise those who do right. For it is God's will that by doing right you should silence the

---

10. It should be noted that some translations and interpretations of this passage render Paul's advice to slaves quite differently: "If you can gain your freedom, do so." But such renderings seem less consistent with the thrust of the passage, which is socially conservative—to a degree that many of us moderns find deeply troubling, to be sure.

ignorance of the foolish. As servants of God, live as free people, yet do not use your freedom as a pretext for evil. Honor everyone. Love the family of believers. Fear God. Honor the emperor.

1 Peter 2:12–17

Missionaries of every era and locale often have practiced this policy. There was no point in undertaking a quixotic crusade against a deeply entrenched social evil when the church was tiny and young. Better to grow the church and then permeate society with gospel values, with the long-term hope of ameliorating or even revolutionizing what was wrong.[11]

Yet we would also expect to see evidence of the kingdom "already" here, in the early church, and in every church. At least within Christian homes and churches—those institutions over which Christians would have the most immediate and extensive control—we would expect to see kingdom values at work overcoming oppression, eliminating inequality, binding disparate people together in love and mutual respect, and the like. We would expect to hear teaching that envisioned that great day when all such barriers to human fellowship and flourishing are done away. We would expect, in short, to catch glimpses of the kingdom and to feel its unstoppable momentum toward universal shalom, even while we also appreciate the way the Holy Spirit skillfully and patiently guides the church to make the most of whatever opportunities it has in this or that situation. In many homes and churches, past and present, we see exactly that sort of evidence of God's "kingdom come."

11. To be sure, some missionaries saw opportunities right away to campaign against social evils. One thinks of Mary Slessor rescuing twins in West Africa and Amy Carmichael rescuing orphans in India as heroic cases in point. But these instances seem to prove the general rule: One does what one can to resist social evils but not at the cost of the gospel proclamation itself, and particularly not in a hopeless and ineffective crusade for social revolution. (Note that my adjectives are leaving open the possibility of a *hopeful* and *effective* crusade when circumstances permit it.) There are several biographies of Mary Slessor and works by and about Amy Carmichael in print. For the history of missions, see the standard if now somewhat outdated Kenneth Scott Latourette, *A History of the Expansion of Christianity*, 7 vols. (New York: Harper & Brothers, 1937–45); and Stephen Neill, *A History of Christian Missions* (London: Penguin, 1964).

Liberty

The apostle Paul gives us paradoxical wisdom on "making the most of the time" in his teaching on Christian liberty (Eph. 5:16; cf. Col. 4:5). First, he asserts a radical freedom in Christ—freedom from law, freedom from social divisions, freedom from religious tradition, freedom even from the world, the flesh, and the devil. Paul's language can hardly be excelled in its breathtaking scope:

> If, because of the one man's trespass, death exercised dominion through that one, much more surely will those who receive the abundance of grace and the free gift of righteousness exercise dominion in life through the one man, Jesus Christ. . . .
>
> For the wages of sin is death, but the free gift of God is eternal life in Christ Jesus our Lord. . . .
>
> For the law of the Spirit of life in Christ Jesus has set you free from the law of sin and of death.
>
> Romans 5:17; 6:23; 8:2

> Grace to you and peace from God our Father and the Lord Jesus Christ, who gave himself for our sins to set us free from the present evil age, according to the will of our God and Father, to whom be the glory forever and ever. Amen.
>
> Galatians 1:3–5

> For in Christ Jesus you are all children of God through faith. As many of you as were baptized into Christ have clothed yourselves with Christ. There is no longer Jew or Greek, there is no longer slave or free, there is no longer male and female; for all of you are one in Christ Jesus.
>
> Galatians 3:26–28

Paul's teaching is echoed in the Epistle to the Hebrews:

> Since, therefore, the children share flesh and blood, he himself likewise shared the same things, so that through death he might destroy the one who has the power of death, that is, the devil, and free those who all their lives were held in slavery by the fear of death.
>
> 2:14–15

Yet inspired by the same Spirit who opens up this great theme of freedom, Paul locates this freedom in the world as it is now. He counsels the prudent use of this freedom for God's number-one priority: the drawing of women and men to himself, and upward to maturity, as the center of God's plan for global redemption. Thus, Paul teaches the use of Christian liberty in a paradoxical sense: the freedom *not* to enjoy and exploit freedom in this or that respect if such curtailment of liberty would promote the greater good.

> For you were called to freedom, brothers and sisters; only do not use your freedom as an opportunity for self-indulgence, but through love become slaves to one another. For the whole law is summed up in a single commandment, "You shall love your neighbor as yourself."
>
> Galatians 5:13–14

> But when you thus sin against members of your family, and wound their conscience when it is weak, you sin against Christ. Therefore, if food is a cause of their falling, I will never eat meat, so that I may not cause one of them to fall.
>
> 1 Corinthians 8:12–13

> "All things are lawful," but not all things are beneficial. "All things are lawful," but not all things build up. Do not seek your own advantage, but that of the other.
>
> 1 Corinthians 10:23–24; cf. 1 Peter 2:16

The actions in question are not sinful. If they were, they would simply be forbidden. In fact, Paul's point is that they are generally legitimate in themselves, but they become illegitimate if enjoying them somehow impedes the supreme cause of the spread of the gospel and the edification of the Christian community. Good things, then, are to be foregone in the interest of better things, particularly in the interest of benefiting others rather than oneself.[12]

---

12. John Calvin offers some striking reflections on the theme of Christian liberty and obedience in regard to various scriptural patterns we have considered. "Now it is the duty of Christian people to keep the ordinances that have been

In regard to the subject at hand, in many situations, it would seem best for everyone involved for women to seize the opportunity to be free and whole, not trammeled and reduced by patriarchy. In fact, that is the situation in much of the world today. We all would benefit from the full emancipation of women, and so we all should strive for it. But in many other cases throughout history, and even in some places in the world today, the social disruption of full-fledged feminism may come at too high a price. Disturbed families, churches, and societies may become more hostile toward the Christian religion—and likely with little or no actual gain in freedom for women. Therefore, this difficult and unattractive possibility of using one's liberty to freely constrain oneself continues to confront us.

In this teaching, Paul has in mind the supreme example of Christ:

> Do nothing from selfish ambition or conceit, but in humility regard others as better than yourselves. Let each of you look not

---

established . . . with a free conscience, indeed, without superstition, yet with a pious and ready inclination to obey. . . . What sort of freedom of conscience could there be in such excessive attentiveness and caution? Indeed, it will be very clear when we consider that these are no fixed and permanent sanctions by which we are bound, but outward rudiments for human weakness. Although not all of us need them, we all use them, for we are mutually bound, one to another, to nourish mutual love. This may be recognized in the examples set forth. . . . What? Does religion consist in a woman's shawl, so that it is unlawful for her to go out with a bare head? Is that decree of Paul's concerning silence so holy that it cannot be broken without great offense? . . . Not at all. For if a woman needs such haste to help a neighbor that she cannot stop to cover her head, she does not offend if she runs to her with head uncovered. And there is a place where it is no less proper for her to speak than elsewhere to remain silent. [Calvin, alas, does not specify that former place.] . . . Nevertheless, the established custom of the region, or humanity itself and the rule of modesty, dictate what is to be done or avoided in these matters. In them a man commits no crime if out of imprudence or forgetfulness he departs from them. . . . Similarly, the days themselves, the hours, the structure of the places of worship, what psalms are to be sung on what day, are matters of no importance. But it is convenient to have definite days and stated hours, and a place suitable to receive all, if there is any concern for the preservation of peace. For confusion in such details would become the seed of great contentions if every man were allowed, as he pleased, to change matters affecting public order!" (*Institutes of the Christian Religion*, ed. John T. McNeill, trans. Ford Lewis Battles [Philadelphia: Westminster, 1960], IV.x.31).

to your own interests, but to the interests of others. Let the same mind be in you that was in Christ Jesus, who, though he was in the form of God, did not regard equality with God as something to be exploited, but emptied himself, taking the form of a slave, being born in human likeness. And being found in human form, he humbled himself and became obedient to the point of death—even death on a cross.

Philippians 2:3–8

Egalitarians properly rejoice in the liberty from oppression and particularly from patriarchy that is won for us in Christ. Freedom from gender discrimination is an important implication of the gospel. Yet we should at least sometimes forgo this particular liberty, among many others, in favor of the greater liberty given to us to do whatever is necessary to further the most fundamental message of the gospel: deliverance from sin and death, reconciliation to God, and enjoyment of eternal life. This is because, for the Christian individual and the Christian church, the question of gender is not just about gender. It is not even primarily about gender. It is about the kingdom of God because *everything* is about the kingdom of God. And because everything is about the kingdom of God, then questions about gender need to be asked in this one, primary context: What will best advance the kingdom of God?

Gift, Calling, Order, and Edification

In looking at the New Testament's teaching about the crucial spheres of home and church, we find four intertwining principles: gift, calling, order, and edification. Paul provides the most teaching on these matters, and his most extensive passage is 1 Corinthians 11–14.

Paul here is concerned with the proper balancing of Christian values. He is delighted that the Corinthians want to participate in the life of the church, but he wants them to do so according to their genuine abilities. Thus, he teaches that each Christian is gifted by the Holy Spirit, and we should discern just how we are gifted and then go on to play our appropriate role in the body of Christ. Indeed, God calls each of us to this or that role at this or that time. "Vocation" is not just for clergy but for everyone.

Paul proceeds to explain that Christians best obey God's call and use their gifts when there is appropriate order in the church. Cacophony may be exciting, but there is no way for one Christian to help another—Paul uses the expression "build up" or "edify" another—when they cancel out each other. So Paul simply asks that people let one another serve in turn, according to their gifts. He forbids the nonsense and the chaos that stem from a selfish desire to enjoy one's own spirituality regardless of the benefit it may or may not bring to the other members of the church.

Do We See Egalitarianism Here or Not?

Do we see egalitarianism here? No, we don't. At least, not obviously. In truth, it is abundantly clear that there are hierarchies in the church and in the home in the pages of the New Testament. The complementarians are simply right about that:

* Elders rule the church, and others follow (Acts 15; 1 Tim. 5:17; 1 Pet. 5:1–5).
* Masters in the home give the orders, and slaves comply (Eph. 6:5–9; Col. 3:22–25; 1 Tim. 6:1–2; Titus 2:9–10; 1 Pet. 2:18).
* Parents instruct, and children obey (Eph. 6:1–4; Col. 3:20–21; 1 Tim. 3:4–5, 12).
* Men teach and exercise authority in the church, while women do not, and husbands are the heads of their wives, while their wives submit to them (1 Cor. 11:1–10; 14:34–35; Eph. 5:22–33; Col. 3:18–19; 1 Tim. 2:11–12; 1 Pet. 3:1–7).

I pause here to recognize that I am contending for an egalitarian position, and yet I apparently have just given away the biblical store! To see whether I can restore any plausibility to my claim to feminism, let's look at the church situation first, and then we will examine the domestic sphere.

The Church

Paul means just what he says about gender, but I mean this in a radical way: He means *everything* he says about gender, not just the favorite passages cited by one side or another.

So how can Paul sound so egalitarian sometimes and so complementarian—even simply patriarchal—at other times? Paul is guided by the Holy Spirit—even used by the Holy Spirit without his full awareness of the implications—to do two things simultaneously: (1) to give the church prudent instruction as to how to survive and thrive in a patriarchal culture that he thinks will not last long; and (2) to maintain and promote the egalitarian dynamic already at work in the career of Jesus that in due course will leave gender lines behind. This doubleness in Paul—which we can see also in the ministry of Jesus—helps to explain why egalitarians and complementarians both find support for their views in Paul's writings. It is this doubleness that is the key to this paradigm on gender.

Even in his own setting, Paul believes that women should keep silent in church *and* that they should pray and prophesy. How can they do both? By being silent at the right times, and by praying and prophesying at the right times. Look at the matter in the discussion of which Paul prescribes silence for women. It is in regard to corporate worship: "When you come together, each one has a hymn, a lesson, a revelation, a tongue, or an interpretation. Let all things be done for building up" (1 Cor. 14:26). Women in this culture, as in most cultures in the history of the world, generally were not educated beyond the domestic arts. Furthermore, they were not socialized into the discourse of formal, public learning. Therefore, in the enthusiasm of their Christian liberty, in the excitement of the freedom found in their full acceptance into the church alongside men, it appears that some women disrupted the meetings with inappropriate questions and other unedifying talk. So Paul tells them, as a general principle, to ask their husbands questions at home—implying the imperative, to be sure, that the husbands have paid attention to the teaching and can answer those questions!

As in all the churches of the saints, women should be silent in
the churches. For they are not permitted to speak, but should be
subordinate, as the law also says. If there is anything they desire to
know, let them ask their husbands at home.

1 Corinthians 14:33–35[13]

Likewise with leadership: Women were not trained to exercise
public leadership over mixed groups, and society would have been

13. Some egalitarian commentators have suggested that this text does not
represent Paul's view but is in fact a scribal gloss, a quotation of a theological
enemy, or some other kind of non-Pauline interpolation. Chief among these
contemporary commentators is Gordon Fee (*The First Epistle to the Corinthians*
[Grand Rapids: Eerdmans, 1990], 699–705). The late F. F. Bruce concurred with
Fee (W. Ward Gasque and Laurel Gasque, "F. F. Bruce: A Mind for What Matters," *Christianity Today* 33 [April 7, 1989]: 24–25). When Gordon Fee and F. F.
Bruce speak on textual matters, we should listen, but I am not yet persuaded.
Even if I were so persuaded, however, it remains that dispensing with this text
does not solve the several other challenges facing egalitarians in Paul's writings.
I am grateful for excellent technical biblical scholarship, but I have come to
conclude that only a *theological* take on these matters will avail. Resorting to
finely argued revisionist technical scholarship—such as endless wranglings over
the meaning of *head* in 1 Corinthians 11 or the interpretation of 1 Timothy 2 in
light of local religious controversies regarding women teachers (e.g., Richard
Clark Kroeger and Catherine Clark Kroeger, *I Suffer Not a Woman: Rethink-
ing 1 Timothy 2:11–15 in the Light of Ancient Evidence* [Grand Rapids: Baker,
1998]; and Linda L. Belleville, "Teaching and Usurping Authority: 1 Timothy
2:11–15," in *Discovering Biblical Equality: Complementarity without Hierarchy*,
ed. Ronald W. Pierce, Rebecca Merrill Groothuis, and Gordon D. Fee, 205–23
[Downers Grove, IL: InterVarsity, 2004])—seems to miss the patriarchal forest
of the entire Bible for particular textual trees. Even if a particular text is shown
to mean something other than what the church has understood it to mean for
centuries, a great deal more patriarchy remains in the Bible.

Furthermore, this marshaling of technical textual and historical scholarship
raises the question of the providence of God. Why would God allow such confusion to continue in the church's reading of these passages for two thousand
years, only to have it resolved in our own day—and then only by considerable
exegetical heavy lifting? It is possible that God so arranged things to facilitate the
church's accommodation of patriarchy until such a time as society was prepared
to entertain egalitarianism. At that time, in a wonderful coincidence, God then
enlightened Bible scholars about the identity of this interpolated text or that
special context, thus facilitating egalitarianism. I think it more likely, however,
and a simpler explanation, that these specially controverted texts are consistent
with Paul's teaching on gender—indeed, with the Bible's teaching in general. I
have suggested, therefore, an alternative egalitarian treatment of these texts.

scandalized by it. So Paul forbids it in the name of gospel priorities. Indeed, one of Paul's most direct teachings about the silence and subordination of women, in 1 Timothy 2:11–15, is preceded in that chapter by this very context of causing as little scandal as possible in order to bring glory to God and particularly to advantage both evangelism and the ongoing edification of believers:

> First of all, then, I urge that supplications, prayers, intercessions, and thanksgivings be made for everyone, for kings and all who are in high positions, so that we may lead a quiet and peaceable life in all godliness and dignity. This is right and is acceptable in the sight of God our Savior, who desires everyone to be saved and to come to the knowledge of the truth.
>
> 1 Timothy 2:1–4

Public prayer and prophecy, however, do not require formal education, and therefore Paul not only allows but simply *expects* women to engage in such edifying discourse. Thus, his only advice to them on this matter is again to avoid unnecessary scandal—remember, Paul never minds causing scandal when the heart of the gospel is at stake—and therefore to dress as their culture expects them to, with their heads covered as a sign of conventional submission to patriarchy:

> But I want you to understand that Christ is the head of every man, and the husband is the head of his wife, and God is the head of Christ. Any man who prays or prophesies with something on his head disgraces his head, but any woman who prays or prophesies with her head unveiled disgraces her head—it is one and the same thing as having her head shaved. For if a woman will not veil herself, then she should cut off her hair; but if it is disgraceful for a woman to have her hair cut off or to be shaved, she should wear a veil. For a man ought not to have his head veiled, since he is the image and reflection of God; but woman is the reflection of man.
>
> 1 Corinthians 11:3–7

Yet it is intriguing, and suggestive, that Paul's teaching about gifts and roles in the church is never sorted into gender-specific categories. He never says that all the leaders, all the pastors, all the teachers, and all the evangelists should be men and that women's gifts reside among the remainder. Furthermore, if I am correct in suggesting that Paul—and God—is not forbidding women from leadership forever and in every circumstance but is instead temporarily accommodating himself to what appears to be the global reality of patriarchy, then we might catch a glimpse of exceptions in the record.[14] We would see anomalies that do not make sense unless they are, indeed, blessed hints of what *could* be and *will* be eventually in the fully present kingdom of God.

We would expect, perhaps, to see exceptional women actually teaching adult men—and we do, in someone such as Priscilla, who instructs even the gifted Apollos. We might see exceptional women offering leadership through their social standing and wealth, as Lydia does, hosting the local church in her home. We might even see exceptional women bearing the titles of eminent leaders in the church, such as "deacon" and "apostle," and we do: "I commend to you our sister Phoebe, a deacon of the church at Cenchreae. . . . Greet Andronicus and Junia [a female name], my relatives who were in prison with me; they are prominent among the apostles" (Rom. 16:1, 7).[15]

We see the same pattern in church history. Patriarchy is the rule, but exceptional movements and individuals keep emerging

14. There has been considerable controversy in anthropological circles about whether there have been, or are today, cultures that can properly be called either matriarchal or egalitarian. I am not an expert in this discourse, but my latest sounding of it indicates that the case for the existence of matriarchies is badly embattled, and the case for egalitarian societies has not won the day. Especially since our own culture has become officially egalitarian, however, there seems to be no reason to preclude the possibility that other societies may have espoused this ideal. It is grimly fascinating, to be sure, that so few have done so, if any have at all.

15. Gordon Fee observes: "The well-known sociology of Macedonia corroborates this [pattern]. . . . Macedonia was well-known as an exception to the norm; from way back women held significant positions in public life. It is therefore not surprising that evidence of their leadership in the church turns up in Philippi" ("Gender Issues: Reflections on the Perspective of the Apostle Paul," in *Christian Perspectives on Gender, Sexuality, and Community,* ed. Maxine Hancock [Vancouver, BC: Regent College Publishing, 2003], 75).

to remind us that patriarchy is a temporary condition and that women can indeed lead, teach, and do everything else a man can do in home and church: female prophets, learned nuns, powerful abbesses, influential authors, effective missionaries, successful evangelists, and, in our day, eminent pastors and theological scholars.

What does this stream of exceptional women tell us? It might tell us that God is willing to use women if men do not make themselves available for his service. Some complementarians have argued this way:

> When so many ministers of the stronger and wiser sex are useless or worse than useless in the work of soul saving, and preach for years without being instrumental in a single conversion, is there not a case for woman's ministry? . . . [Yet] had Barak better played the man, Deborah had better played the woman. . . . Had the disciples tarried longer at the sepulchre, Mary need not have been the first proclaimer of our Lord.[16]

This record of women's public ministry, however, could be interpreted instead as squaring nicely with the paradigm offered here. Where society will not tolerate anything but patriarchy, then the church accommodates itself to that unhappy reality for the greater good of spreading the gospel and, indeed, of simply surviving under the threat of persecution. But where society has

---

Having positively cited Gordon Fee, I now must register an important disagreement we have concerning this question. He believes "'praying and prophesying' to be not exclusive of other forms of ministry but representative of ministry in general. And since 'prophets' precedes 'teachers' in the ranking in 1 Corinthians 12:28 and prophesying is grouped with teaching, revelation and knowledge in 1 Corinthians 14:6, one may legitimately assume that women and men together shared in all these expressions of Spirit gifting, including teaching, in the gathered assembly" (Gordon D. Fee, "Praying and Prophesying in the Assemblies," in *Discovering Biblical Equality,* 149). One may *not* "legitimately assume" such a generalization. Paul is distinguishing among modes of speech that he sees as appropriate and inappropriate for women in church gatherings. Thus, he provides a general rule and also suggestive exceptions in various epistles.

16. L. E. Maxwell, "The Weaker Sex," *Prairie Overcomer* 39 (April 1966): 130. Many others have argued this in our own day as well. For more instances, see my *Evangelical Landscapes,* 128–31.

open spaces in which Christian women can flourish, they have flourished and still do.[17]

To put it more pointedly: When society was patriarchal, as it was in the New Testament context and as it has been everywhere in the world except in modern society in our day, the church avoided scandal by going along with it—fundamentally evil as patriarchy was and is. Now, however, that modern society is at least officially egalitarian, the scandal is that the church is *not* going along with society, not rejoicing in the unprecedented freedom to let women and men serve according to gift and call without an arbitrary gender line.[18] This scandal impedes both the evangelism of others and the edification—the retention and development of faith—of those already converted.[19]

17. Unless Christians reflexively take one of two extreme positions, namely, that "society is always wrong" or that "society is always right" (roughly congruent with the "Christ against culture" and "Christ of culture" models of H. Richard Niebuhr's classic typology in *Christ and Culture* [New York: Harper & Row, 1951]), then Christians are obliged always to keep assessing whether this or that dynamic of contemporary culture now requires this or that response—whether resistance, affirmation, or something in between. Going along with society is not necessarily a bad thing or necessarily a good thing. It all depends on where society is going and how, as evaluated by gospel priorities.

18. The modern drive for the liberation of women is a secularized form of biblical teaching about the equality of men and women. It is no coincidence that feminism emerges in a Jewish and Christian social context, among all the other cultures of the world. It is also a matter of historical record that many of the early feminists were churchgoing Christians who articulated their cause precisely in biblical terms. There is now a considerable literature on this subject. Pioneering works in the field are Donald W. Dayton, *Discovering an Evangelical Heritage* (San Francisco: Harper & Row, 1976), esp. chap. 8, "The Evangelical Roots of Feminism," 85–98; and Nancy A. Hardesty, *Women Called to Witness: Evangelical Feminism in the Nineteenth Century* (Nashville: Abingdon, 1984). A good bibliography on more recent history and more general themes is Patricia Applebaum, *A Bibliographic Guide to Contemporary Sources*, special bibliographic edition of *Women and Twentieth-Century Protestantism* (Spring 1999).

19. William Webb points out something that is obvious to many in the pews but is too rarely remarked on in the literature: The continuation of patriarchy by churches in this society puts a religious stumbling block in the way of those already converted (*Slaves, Women, and Homosexuals*, 254).

The Home

Readers who have gotten this far may wonder if there is a kind of sleight of hand, or even a sort of theological judo, going on here. I am defending egalitarianism by granting the complementarians almost everything they claim and then replying that gender distinctions are a result of sin in fallen human society, not divinely ordered human relations. Thus, such distinctions are practiced in the church only as a kind of desperate expedient, an accommodation to our hard hearts that is to be done away with when the time is ripe. I then argue that this time has come, not because I somehow discern that we are in the end times, as some enthusiastic egalitarians argue, but because I observe that modern society has become ready to accept homes, churches, and secular institutions that welcome women into all roles, including leadership.

How did I come to that sort of conclusion? Why do I think the Holy Spirit counts patriarchy as a sinful, oppressive structure to which he nonetheless accommodated himself and the church until such time as both church and society could do away with it? Because that is what I think the Holy Spirit has already done in one extremely important case: slavery.

The institution of slavery and the institution of patriarchy occur together in at least two key junctures in Christian memory. In nineteenth-century America, abolitionism and feminism were allies for decades—until abolition carried the day (at least officially), and feminists' former allies did not all follow through on the second crusade. Much further back, we encounter slavery and patriarchy again, this time in the pages of the New Testament. Indeed, the social conservatism of the New Testament is exemplified in the linkage of three domestic institutions in several similar passages in the epistles: slavery, marriage, and parent/child relations. In each case, the apostles condone the relationships of their day and then ameliorate each one in light of the gospel. Here is one such passage:

> Wives, be subject to your husbands, as is fitting in the Lord. Husbands, love your wives and never treat them harshly.

Children, obey your parents in everything, for this is your
acceptable duty in the Lord. Fathers, do not provoke your children, or they may lose heart. Slaves, obey your earthly masters in
everything, not only while being watched and in order to please
them, but wholeheartedly, fearing the Lord. . . . Masters, treat
your slaves justly and fairly, for you know that you also have a
Master in heaven.

> Colossians 3:18–22; 4:1;[20] cf. Ephesians 5:21–6:9;
> 1 Peter 2:18–3:7 (although this last text lacks
> the parallel of children and parents)

In the case of slavery, Christians worldwide have come to
agree that the social conservatism of the New Testament was a
temporary matter. The early church probably expected Christ to
return literally at any moment, so it made no sense for slaves to
rise up against masters or for Christians to agitate for slavery's
abolition. Christians enjoyed no possibility of success in such
a cause, given their tiny numbers. And Christ was coming back
to do away with such things momentarily anyhow.

As the church accommodated itself over the centuries to the
so-called delay of the parousia, or second coming, however, it
gradually began to conclude that the thrust of the Bible regarding the dignity of all people entailed the abolition of slavery. In
the modern period of the Christian West, therefore, for the first
time in history, a society voluntarily rid itself of slavery.[21]

In America, this consensus is officially less than 150 years old,
and the racism that legitimized it has not been eradicated to this
day. Indeed, preachers on both sides of the slavery controversy
marshaled powerful, Bible-based arguments that convinced mil-

---

20. The chapter division between Col. 3:25 and 4:1 gets my vote as one of the
weirdest in the entire Bible.

21. Not all abolitionists were orthodox Christians—or even Christians at all.
But abolitionism in both Britain and America did feature Christians in the vanguard. Also, the broader cultural matrix in which slavery was raised as something
to be discussed, not taken for granted, and then finally destroyed was produced
by the defining religion of that society, Christianity—even as offshoots of and
reactions to it (such as various forms of deism and liberalism) also contributed
to the cause. For recent reflections on this point, see Rodney Stark, *For the Glory
of God: How Monotheism Led to Reformation, Science, Witch-Hunts, and the End
of Slavery* (Princeton: Princeton University Press, 2003), chap. 4.

lions of believers. Some fair-minded observers have concluded that the proslavery forces had the better of this debate, since a straightforward interpretation of the passages regarding slavery conveys no obvious condemnation of the institution and seems instead to encourage Christians in both roles, master and slave, to stay right where they are and simply to behave properly.[22] Yet there is no important Christian leader anywhere in the modern world today who defends slavery. Not one.

What about the parent/child relationship? Surely no one would suggest that children ought to disobey their parents and that parents are free to abuse their children. But no one should suggest, likewise, that children are in perpetual thrall to their parents' commands. The parent/child relationship is a temporary one that accomplishes certain things and then is outgrown as the child no longer needs his parents' direction. Indeed, Genesis 2:24 makes it quite clear that part of normal adulthood involves leaving father and mother and taking on the parental role oneself in a new household.

The same dynamic is true in the husband/wife relationship. In a social situation in which the husband has more power—social, intellectual, political, and financial—because patriarchal society has awarded it to him simply on the basis of his sex, he should use that power self-givingly to benefit his wife, as Christ uses his superior power on behalf of the church, his spouse. Therefore, Paul's extended treatment of husband/wife relations in Ephesians 5 begins with the call to mutual submission, and then (in what seems to some today to be a contradiction) he exhorts women to submit to their husbands, and men to care for their wives, in parallel with the relationship of Christ and the church:

> Be subject to one another out of reverence for Christ.
> Wives, be subject to your husbands as you are to the Lord. For the husband is the head of the wife just as Christ is the head of

22. See E. Brooks Holifield, *Theology in America: Christian Thought from the Age of the Puritans to the Civil War* (New Haven: Yale University Press, 2003); and especially Mark A. Noll, *America's God: From Jonathan Edwards to Abraham Lincoln* (New York: Oxford University Press, 2002).

the church, the body of which he is the Savior. Just as the church
is subject to Christ, so also wives ought to be, in everything, to
their husbands.

Husbands, love your wives, just as Christ loved the church and
gave himself up for her, in order to make her holy by cleansing her
with the washing of water by the word, so as to present the church
to himself in splendor, without a spot or wrinkle or anything of the
kind—yes, so that she may be holy and without blemish. In the same
way, husbands should love their wives as they do their own bodies.
He who loves his wife loves himself. For no one ever hates his own
body, but he nourishes and tenderly cares for it, just as Christ does
for the church, because we are members of his body. "For this reason
a man will leave his father and mother and be joined to his wife, and
the two will become one flesh." This is a great mystery, and I am
applying it to Christ and the church. Each of you, however, should
love his wife as himself, and a wife should respect her husband.

Ephesians 5:21–33

This is exactly the pattern of all Paul's exhortations: Do not try to
change what cannot be changed, such as patriarchy or slavery,
but make the best of it according to all that we know of mutual
love in Christ.

In a society such as ours, in which patriarchy is no longer
everywhere assumed, it is not at all clear just what Ephesians
5 says about gender hierarchy in the family. It is clear enough,
one supposes, that wives are to "be subject" to their husbands,
but what does that entail?

No complementarian scholar seriously advises that husbands
make all decisions in domestic life. Some popular preachers might
say so, but they do not realize that such absolute authority and
responsibility did not reside in the husband in the ancient world
either: Wives had a considerable voice in the domestic sphere. Does
it mean that the husband sets the family policies, perhaps with
the advice of his wife, and then she, as a good subordinate, carries
them out? Perhaps that is what it means, but it is difficult to find
complementarian scholars who will argue even this position.

I recognize that in many Christian homes the husband and
father wields supreme authority. I recognize that even in more
moderate homes the symbols of authority reside in the male: He

leads the conversations, he leads in family worship, he administers discipline, he has the final say in any important decision, and so on. I recognize also the implicit devaluing of women's competence and authority in such situations. I am not claiming, therefore, that a complementarian position, even a relatively mild one, does not make a difference. What I am arguing at present is that in the *scholarly* literature one rarely finds defenders of such lopsided patriarchy.

Instead, one finds complementarians telling husbands to make sure they love their wives self-sacrificially, as Christ loves the church. Such exposition is welcome, to be sure, but we must notice that it avoids the point at issue: It does not help us "cash out" the difference between a loving complementarian marriage and an equally loving egalitarian one. In fact, the only common application of genuine gender distinction in marriage found in the complementarian literature today is the "breaking the deadlock" hypothetical: If the mutually respectful husband and wife cannot come to a decision together that needs to be made, then the husband is to cast the deciding vote.

Such a reading of this passage strikes me as ludicrous. If Paul, a master of the Greek language, had intended this idea, then surely he could have been more plain about it! Furthermore, when I have asked complementarian couples how often in years or even decades of marriage they have had to resort to this device, the answer invariably comes back the same: Never. So are we really supposed to think that the Holy Spirit inspired the apostle Paul to write something that is never actually applicable?[23]

It is better to see this passage in parallel with slaveholding and parenting. Society has already awarded power to masters, parents, and husbands. Paul does not advise a domestic revolution that would upset all these relationships. Instead, he commands the amelioration of these exercises of power. Along the

23. For a fascinating sociological corroboration of the foregoing, see Christian Smith, "Male Headship and Gender Equality," in *Christian America? What Evangelicals Really Want* (Berkeley: University of California Press, 2000), 160–91. See also W. Bradford Wilcox, *Soft Patriarchs, New Men: How Christianity Shapes Fathers and Husbands* (Chicago: University of Chicago Press, 2004).

way, the Holy Spirit inspires him to plant seeds of emancipation that blossom when the time is right.[24]

Another notorious passage regarding gender can be understood in the same way. The apostle Peter describes women as the "weaker sex"—or, in the King James Version's memorable rendering, the "weaker vessel" (1 Pet. 3:7). But it is not clear that Peter is suggesting something universal and necessary about women, something essential about them, as if all women everywhere and always are weaker than all men. Indeed, that seems to be obvious nonsense. What is not nonsensical is that in a patriarchal society Peter is telling the simple truth: Economically, politically, legally, educationally—when it comes to social power—women *are* weaker than men.[25] Therefore, he advises the Christian wife

24. John Howard Yoder is among many scholars who note that "for a first-century husband to love (*agapan*) his wife, or for a first-century father to avoid angering his child, or for a first-century master to deal with his servant in the awareness that they are both slaves to a higher master, is to make a more concrete and more sweeping difference in the way that husband or father or master behaves than the other imperative of subordination would have made practically in the behavior of the wife or child or servant" (*Politics of Jesus*, 181–82). I. Howard Marshall also asks us to take Paul's individuality seriously, as a particular man in a particular time and place: "Paul should not be expected to step outside his time and see the consequences of his teaching any more than he is to be faulted for not commanding the abolition of slavery or the development of universal suffrage" ("Mutual Love and Submission in Marriage," in *Discovering Biblical Equality*, 195).

25. David Scholer provides this capsule description: "In the Mediterranean world of the first century the overwhelming perception about women was that they were inferior, that they ought to stay at home, that they ought to be submissive, that they ought to be silent, that they ought never to speak in public, and that they should have no role of leadership of any kind. Wives were to be subject to their husbands 'in everything.'

"In general, the ancient Greco-Roman Mediterranean society was structured basically as follows. The average age of a man at marriage was thirty, but the average age of a woman was eighteen or less at marriage. When a man married he was already a man of the world who knew how to live in society. He was a person who could function socially and economically. When a woman married she was still a girl who had never even been allowed to answer a knock at the front door of her home. A typical woman bore a child about every two years or thirty months through her childbearing years. She was always 'barefoot and pregnant' and at home. She bore a child as soon as the previous one was weaned. Although many of them died, that was her lot. Further, women generally had no education beyond the domestic arts" (David M. Scholer, "Feminist Hermeneutics and Evangelical Biblical Interpretation," *Journal of the Evangelical Theological Society* 30 [December 1987]: 416).

to play her role well and to expect her husband to play his, to their mutual benefit.

Let us be sure to note that Peter exhorts the wife to be submissive precisely because of gospel priorities and, we can fairly assume, because he recognizes that marriage conventions of his time are not ready to be altered in any radically egalitarian way. What he does *not* say is that wives should submit to their husbands because he believes in some sort of "essential" submissiveness supposedly endemic to being a woman: "Wives, in the same way, accept the authority of your husbands, so that, even if some of them do not obey the word, they may be won over without a word by their wives' conduct, when they see the purity and reverence of your lives" (1 Pet. 3:1–2; cf. Titus 2:4–5).

A Suggestive Pattern of Doubleness?

Since we are taking on the most difficult texts for egalitarians, let us consider a suggestive pattern that appears in one of the most difficult texts in the Old Testament and recurs in a number of the most difficult texts in the New:

> The LORD spoke to Moses, saying: Speak to the people of Israel, saying: If a woman conceives and bears a male child, she shall be ceremonially unclean seven days; as at the time of her menstruation, she shall be unclean. On the eighth day the flesh of his foreskin shall be circumcised. Her time of blood purification shall be thirty-three days; she shall not touch any holy thing, or come into the sanctuary, until the days of her purification are completed. If she bears a female child, she shall be unclean two weeks, as in her menstruation; her time of blood purification shall be sixty-six days.
>
> Leviticus 12:1–5

There are at least two major matters here from a feminist point of view. First, it appears that menstruation and bearing children—two of the experiences of womanhood that are glorified in much feminist literature—are disparaged in the Bible. Indeed, they are forms of impurity that require temporary quarantine. Yet a few chapters later, in Leviticus 15, it appears that the matter is not the uncleanness of a woman but of any human body that discharges fluids. The man who has an otherwise-undescribed discharge is likewise unclean, as is the man who has a seminal discharge. Scholars assure us that there is no sexism here. The matter at stake is the common ancient Near Eastern concern for ritual purity, not a disparagement of women's bodies.

The second matter is the disparate time required for purification in the case of a male child versus a female child. The latter is twice that of the former, in the case of both personal uncleanness and so-called blood purification. Doesn't this indicate that the Torah sees men as twice as important as women?

There is no doubt that the Torah is a patriarchal text. Men have legal, political, and economic power over women, children, slaves, animals, lands—everything. But two observations must also be made. First, the Torah is not, in Christian eyes, God's ultimate word on human society. Old Testament scholar Iain Provan illuminates this point:

> The law must always be read in the context of the creation purposes of God, because Old Testament law seems to be aimed at dealing often with ugly reality as it is, rather than enunciating ideal principles of conduct. That is what modern law does, too. It does not prescribe virtue; it deals with ugly reality as it actually is. . . . [The laws regarding men and women are] attempts to regulate what otherwise would be even worse situations for the woman concerned.[26]

Jesus reminds his Jewish audience of that in his preaching, as he cautions that much of the Torah was accommodated to the sinfulness of Israel and that he is now calling Israel to a much higher standard of righteousness:

> Some Pharisees came to him, and to test him they asked, "Is it lawful for a man to divorce his wife for any cause?" He answered, "Have you not read that the one who made them at the beginning 'made them male and female,' and said, 'For this reason a man

26. Iain W. Provan, "Why Bother with the Old Testament Regarding Gender and Sexuality?" in *Christian Perspectives on Gender, Sexuality, and Community*, 40.

shall leave his father and mother and be joined to his wife, and the two shall become one flesh'? So they are no longer two, but one flesh. Therefore what God has joined together, let no one separate." They said to him, "Why then did Moses command us to give a certificate of dismissal and to divorce her?" He said to them, "It was because you were so hard-hearted that Moses allowed you to divorce your wives, but from the beginning it was not so. And I say to you, whoever divorces his wife, except for unchastity, and marries another commits adultery."

Matthew 19:3–9

The patriarchy of the Torah, therefore, is not to be understood by the church as a blueprint for Christian conduct. It is to be read as Scripture, yes—as "inspired by God and . . . useful for teaching, for reproof, for correction, and for training in righteousness" (2 Tim. 3:16). But just *how* it is useful for us is a question of careful hermeneutics. My sense is that these sorts of passages in the Torah are illustrative of God's accommodation to something he does not like, namely, patriarchy, and thus also his simultaneous amelioration of it, for scholars indicate that the treatment of women in the law is no worse, and frequently better, than the ancient Near Eastern parallels.[27]

The second observation to be made about the Torah leads us to the intriguing pattern of doubleness seen in similar New Testament texts: the customary privileging of the male in the same context as a perhaps surprising affirmation of male and female as equal.

Let's begin with the Leviticus passage about childbirth. Yes, bearing a female child renders the mother ceremonially impure for twice as long as if she had borne a male child. But the passage quoted above goes on as follows:

> When the days of her purification are completed, *whether for a son or for a daughter,* she shall bring to the priest at the entrance of the tent of meeting a lamb in its first year for a burnt offering, and a pigeon or a turtledove for a sin offering. He shall offer it before the LORD, and make atonement on her behalf; then she

---

27. To this vast subject, a helpful introduction is provided in ibid., 25–41.

shall be clean from her flow of blood. This is the law for her who bears a child, *male or female.*

Leviticus 12:6–7, emphasis added

Another highly problematic example is Exodus 21 regarding male and female slaves, but it has a similar pattern. It is too long to quote here, but it is a complex interweaving of both the standard privileging of men and the affirmation of men and women as equal (including male and female slaves and children).

Some key New Testament texts contain a similar pattern of doubleness regarding gender. As Paul is wrapping up his discussion of head coverings in 1 Corinthians 11, he concludes in patriarchal style:

> For a man ought not to have his head veiled, since he is the image and reflection of God; but woman is the reflection of man. Indeed, man was not made from woman, but woman from man. Neither was man created for the sake of woman, but woman for the sake of man. For this reason a woman ought to have a symbol of authority on her head, because of the angels.

verses 7–10

I shall not tackle verse 10, since it is much controverted and not especially illuminating. But the rest seems pretty typical of a first-century rabbi who is reading Genesis 1 and 2 through patriarchal lenses—lenses not all of us share. Indeed, as many Bible scholars have pointed out, Paul's interpretation of woman as the reflection of man, and not directly of God as his image, seems to fly in the face of Genesis 1:26–27. His depiction of the second creation story, that of Genesis 2, of the woman being created from and for the man seems a bit tendentious. The *adam* was not obviously sexed before the division into male and female, the rejoining of which division is clearly in view in the "two become one flesh" vision of marriage at the end of that chapter. The woman is created as a partner, an *ezer.* This word is usually translated "helper" and is used generally in the Old Testament of God himself as "helper" of his people. Thus, the fundamental concept is of partnership and useful companionship for the man, not of a subordinate to the man. Similar problems emerge in exegeting the 1 Timothy 2 passage: "For Adam was formed first, then Eve; and Adam was not deceived, but the woman was deceived and became a transgressor" (vv. 13–14). Again, Paul ignores Genesis 1, in which male and female are created at the same time as the image of God together. Then we see that his argument from Genesis 2 that the prior creation of the man entails some sort of *political* superiority seems not to be taught in Genesis 2 itself.[28]

As for verse 14, Paul may seem to be suggesting that all women are more prone to spiritual deception than all men, and thus they should be silent in church. But this interpretation seems preposterous coming from a man with such obvious regard for Priscilla and numerous other wise women in the church whom he gladly affirms by name (see the greetings in Rom. 16).

It is no light thing, of course, to question the apostle Paul—and especially when these texts are Holy Scripture! But just

28. Some scholars suggest that Adam's naming of his wife as "woman" in Genesis 2 parallels his naming of the animals earlier and that he is to be understood as "in charge" of all that he names. The passage does not say, in fact, that his naming of the animals means that he is in charge: God put human beings (male and female) in charge explicitly in the creation mandate of Genesis 1. But even if there is such hierarchical significance to assigning names, Genesis 2 is not unequivocally on the side of patriarchalists. Adam's recognition of the woman as "woman"—it is not said that he "names" her—can be argued instead in egalitarian terms: that he sees her as "just like me" and simply uses the correct term for this phenomenon. That is what *ishshah* means vis-à-vis the term for the man himself, *ish*. Neither of these terms is a name. Adam's proper naming of his wife as Eve does not take place until after the fall and therefore may be a sign of patriarchy emerging from the fall. Thus, the argument from naming can be seen as supporting egalitarianism even as it has traditionally been seen as supporting patriarchy. No side obviously wins this one, and since the passage itself does not connect naming with either equality or hierarchy—nor does any other biblical text do so—I do not count it for much.

For a delightful change in rhetorical style from the way these issues are usually discussed, see Alvera Mickelsen, "Does Order of Creation, Redemption, and Climax Demand Female Supremacy? A Satire," appendix 1, in Gretchen Gaebelein Hull, *Equal to Serve: Women and Men in the Church and Home* (Old Tappan, NJ: Revell, 1987), 245–50.

what to make of Paul's deployment of these brief, allusive, and ad hoc arguments—rather than what he says in his extended reflections—is a vexed area of hermeneutical scholarship,[29] and upon it I can shed no definitive light. So I concede that it is easy to read some of these verses as supporting patriarchy everywhere and always, but I also maintain that one does not have to read them that way. And I remind my complementarian friends that the task is to make sense of *all* that Paul says, including the apparently egalitarian verses, some of which appear *in the same passage.*

Can we somehow avoid becoming mired in these questions? Perhaps we can, if we first concede that Paul is maintaining a patriarchal line, whatever one makes of his arguments for it, and if we then go on to notice what Paul says immediately following his argument in 1 Corinthians 11: "Nevertheless, in the Lord woman is not independent of man or man independent of woman. For just as woman came from man, so man comes through woman; but all things come from God" (vv. 11–12). Paul follows the same double pattern we saw in the Torah: He affirms some sort of patriarchal conduct, but then he also affirms equality in a way that provides the grounds for egalitarianism.

Consider also the long passage in Ephesians 5 about husbands and wives in which this pattern is inverted. I need to say at the outset that I have trouble buying the common egalitarian argument about this passage, namely, that Paul is really saying the same thing in two ways. Egalitarians often suggest that he is teaching husbands and wives to treat each other equally and identically but using different language in each case—as if perhaps he is pulling wives up from their degradation with one hand and pulling down husbands from their position of false power with the other. If this is what Paul is saying, he seems to have

---

29. Consider also that no major Christian body applies the strictures regarding widowhood that Paul outlines in the same epistle that complementarians invoke regarding the restriction of female leadership and public speaking: 1 Timothy 5:3–16. Egalitarians thus want to ask why 1 Timothy 2:11–15 is "timeless" and 1 Timothy 5:3–16 is so easily ignored: Is it really just because Paul invokes Genesis 2 in the former case but not in the latter? Egalitarians think that is a lot of freight to be carried by a couple of ambiguous allusions.

an oddly roundabout way of putting this simple point—and the Holy Spirit has somehow failed to help the church see that point through two thousand years of Christian domestic patriarchy.

Instead, the parallel Paul draws with Christ and the church—who are not equal in both fact and role—seems to militate against any simple sense of final equivalence. Furthermore, the typical egalitarian argument that Jesus models submission and self-abnegation in his service to the church is true but not true enough. Such a Christology presents a truncated picture: Jesus is also Lord of the church, the one who gives commands to the church and who expects worship from the church, even as he provides self-sacrificially for the church. Thus, Paul is playing off the wonderful paradox of the one who is both Lord and servant of the church in order to provide a splendid model for husbands to love their wives, from whatever may be their analogical positions of social power, with Christlike affection and self-sacrifice.

Having maintained, then, the patriarchal side of the double-ness we keep noticing (albeit an importantly mitigated patri-archy), let us observe the egalitarian side as well, as seen in how the long passage begins: "Be subject to one another out of reverence for Christ" (Eph. 5:21). Indeed, the following passage distinguishing wives and husbands grammatically depends on this verse, which unites them: The verb "be subject" is missing in the Greek text of verse 22, as verse 22 assumes verse 21. Thus, the exhortation to wives to "submit" is linked at the very level of syntax to *mutual* submission.

This double pattern appears again in 1 Peter. It perhaps is worth reviewing this entire passage to see the irrefutable call to conform to patriarchy combined with an incipient egalitarianism:

Wives, in the same way, accept the authority of your husbands, so that, even if some of them do not obey the word, they may be won over without a word by their wives' conduct, when they see the purity and reverence of your lives. Do not adorn yourselves outwardly by braiding your hair, and by wearing gold ornaments or fine clothing; rather, let your adornment be the inner self with the lasting beauty of a gentle and quiet spirit, which is very precious in God's sight. It was in this way long ago that the holy women who hoped in God used to adorn themselves by accepting the authority of their husbands. Thus Sarah obeyed Abraham and called him lord. You have become her daughters as long as you do what is good and never let fears alarm you.

Husbands, in the same way, show consideration for your wives in your life together, paying honor to the woman as the weaker sex, *since they too are also heirs of the gracious gift of life*—so that nothing may hinder your prayers.

3:1–7, emphasis added[30]

What Then?

My complementarian friends may be exasperated at this point. "We don't deny women's equality! We say the sexes are entirely equal and are simply to play different roles. These passages make exactly *our* point, not yours!"

But then we have to consider this question: Why would God call entirely equal sexes to deeply different roles? Why would one role be that of leadership and the other of submission if women and men are equal not only in status and dignity before God but in every other way as well?

Not so long ago in the West, and not so far away in the world even today, patriarchy made sense because it was assumed that women were inferior in ways pertinent to leadership. Women

---

30. Peter Davids puts things rather more sharply than I do, but he is well worth hearing on this point: "When addressing those without power (slaves and wives), [Peter] does not call for revolution but upholds the values of the culture insofar as they do not conflict with commitment to Christ. He then reframes their behavior by removing it from the realm of necessity and giving it a dignity, either that of identification with Christ or of identification with the 'holy women' of Jewish antiquity. When speaking to the ones with power, however, he asks them not to use their power but to treat those they could dominate as their equals—for in fact they are. . . . The question for today is, Will men/husbands try to hold on to an authority over their wives that once was given them by the surrounding culture but now for the most part they no longer have? Or will they gladly drop power, as well as the pretense to power, and treat their wives as equals, reaping not only a more intimate marriage relationship but also divine pleasure?" (Peter H. Davids, "A Silent Witness in Marriage: 1 Peter 3:1–7," in *Discovering Biblical Equality*, 238).

were understood to be less rational, more emotional, less courageous, more sentimental, less objective, more intuitive, and so on. Thus, it made sense for men to dominate and women to submit, just as it made the same sort of sense for white people to dominate everyone else if everyone else was understood to be inferior and even subhuman.[31]

Not many complementarians want to argue that way today, however. Social-scientific arguments show that many women surpass many men in every important respect, from intelligence (however understood) to morality (however understood) to psychological health (however understood) to physical prowess (however understood).[32] However much it can still be generalizable that women are physically smaller than men, there does not seem to be any important respect in which one can make similar generalizations about anything else of importance. So why in a modern society would a broad tendency to greater physical size and strength alone have anything to do with restricting leadership to men in home, church, or anyplace else, even as a general principle? Then—to pursue this logic to absurdity—what about the individual women who are stronger than all the men nearby? Shouldn't they then lead that particular group? Should we be arm wrestling to see who will become the next chief of surgery, or law partner, or bishop?

The complementarian position has become incoherent.[33]

Thanks be to God that many complementarians are *not* sexists

31. To be sure, male leadership made sense only if "leadership" was understood in typically masculine terms. But what if empathy, intuition, relationality, subjectivity, and the like are valued as important ingredients of leadership as well? Then it would follow that even if men and women are stereotyped in this way, it would still be best to enjoy the benefits of women's qualities in leadership as complements to men's.

32. Mary Stewart Van Leeuwen, *Gender and Grace: Love, Work, and Parenting in a Changing World* (Downers Grove, IL: InterVarsity, 1990); and Elaine Storkey, *Origins of Difference: The Gender Debate Revisited* (Grand Rapids: Baker Academic, 2001).

33. Thus, I repudiate even the "ultra-soft patriarchy" mentioned by William Webb, a position I find not only incoherent but also inchoate. I literally do not understand what such a position is, either theoretically or practically. Webb gives us little help in this regard. See Webb, *Slaves, Women, and Homosexuals*, 242–43. To his credit, complementarian champion Dan Doriani recognizes some

who believe that women are inferior to men. (In regard to those who maintain that women really are inferior in these important respects, I will not pause to say much, except that the Bible, reason, and experience are against you. All you have on your side, from a Christian point of view, are misogynist texts scattered here and there in the tradition from the patristic period to our own.) To the complementarians who do believe that women are equal and yet see the Bible as restricting leadership to men, let me respectfully and fraternally ask, Why would God mandate that pattern forever? May I invite you to consider the Bible in the way I am suggesting, which does, I think, make better sense of the elements of both patriarchy and equality that many egalitarians and complementarians agree are present.

My fundamental practical question therefore is this: What are Christians supposed to do when society itself shifts to egalitarianism? There is no longer a rationale for the woman to remain in the culturally expected role of dependence and submission, just as there is no rationale for the grown-up child to act as if he requires his parents' direction as he did when he was young. When, under the providence of God and the ongoing, spreading influence of kingdom values, society opens up to the abolition of slavery or the emancipation of women, then Christians can rejoice and be in the vanguard of such change—as we have been in both causes. The irony remains precisely in Christians lagging behind society and still requiring a submissive role for women, a posture that now is a mirror image of the scandal that egalitarianism would have caused in the patriarchal first century.

This, then, is the paradigm of gender I submit for your consideration. It makes the most sense to me of what for many have

---

of the problems afflicting his position. But he fails to see that even if we come to some widely shared conclusions about essential differences between women and men, complementarianism founders on two shoals: (1) It is unlikely in the extreme that *all* men differ from *all* women in each respect (e.g., analytical ability, empathy with others); and (2) even if that were true, it is absurd to maintain that the leaders of a church—including its teachers and governors—ought to be comprised entirely of one set of traits without the complementary value of the other set. See Dan Doriani, *Women and Ministry: What the Bible Teaches* (Wheaton: Crossway, 2003), 168–74.

appeared to be contradictions in Scripture, in church history, and in life today in the modern world.

The next chapter exposes this proposal to counterarguments of various sorts in order to test it and to see if something better should be said.

3

Responses to Arguments

Because the paradigm I have offered is neither complementarian nor typically egalitarian, it can be challenged from both sides. Let's consider, then, a variety of arguments to see how well this paradigm stands up to such questioning.

As we do so, we will remember one of the principles of theological method established in the first chapter: The task of Christian theology is not to arrive at the one, timeless, seamless answer that fits everything nicely into place without strain and without remainder. The task instead is to formulate an interpretation that does the best job, relative to other options, of explaining most of the most important data and as much of the remainder as possible. The fact, then, that my paradigm does not explain every detail as well as does another interpretation must be acknowledged in the interests of both Christian honesty and the humble openness we all should maintain in hopes of having our ideas improved. If I dismiss a contrary datum or interpretation, explain it away, or otherwise circumvent it, I miss an opportunity to reconsider and reconstruct my interpretation for the better. But the fact that my paradigm does not explain every detail as well as does another interpretation in a particular case does not mean that it isn't the best one overall that is currently available. If it is the best one available, then it is the one we ought to adopt.[1]

I have tried to deal fairly with arguments from particular Scripture passages in the foregoing discussions. Now we can encounter other sorts of arguments: from theology, church history, and contemporary experience and practice.

Arguments from Theology

The relations among members of the Trinity demonstrate how men and women should treat each other.

The first troubling thing to notice here is that this argument is deployed by both complementarians and egalitarians. Complementarians argue that the members of the Trinity are indeed coequal, but the Son and the Spirit willingly submit to the Father, and the Spirit humbly bears witness not to himself but to the Son. Thus, women can submit to men without feeling automatically devalued. Egalitarians argue from the coequality of the members of the Trinity to the opposite conclusion: The members of the Trinity play different roles, but none of them dominates the others. Indeed, they are all involved in all aspects of divine work, from creation through redemption to consummation, in an interplay of mutual joy and cooperation.

The complementarians get the better of this sort of argument. The Father is always pictured in the Bible in the supreme position and never "rotates off" that position for another member of the Trinity. The Son always is pictured as deferring to

---

1. I suppose one might even conclude that two or more options are equally plausible, in which case one is free to select what one prefers, or, perhaps better, to suspend judgment until one emerges as superior. But I should like to think that on an issue of this importance and urgency, one will seek at least a preponderance of warrants on behalf of one particular option and thus embrace it with a degree of confidence.

the Father, and the Spirit is sent by the Father in the name of the Son.[2]

The problem I have with the complementarian reference to the Trinity, then, is that it is a bad theological move—by *anyone*, on *any* side of this issue. For one thing, the Trinity is/are three, but when it comes to gender, we are instead talking about two. For another thing, the Father and the Son are depicted as two males, and even the biblical pronouns for the Spirit are masculine—even though our theology reminds us that God is not actually male.[3] Finally, in Genesis 1, we encounter the introduction of the idea of human beings—male and female—created in the image of God. In this passage, there is no explicit reference to the Trinity at all. Indeed, nowhere in the Bible does an author draw implications from the nature of the Trinity to human relations.

Many theologians (I among them) strongly endorse circumspection when it comes to the theological device of using one of the great mysteries of the faith—the internal life of God in the Trinity—to shed light on another doctrine. Some doctrines do require deployment of the doctrine of the Trinity, most notably Christology, soteriology, and pneumatology. But the question of gender seems to be one of those theological subjects not much improved by reference to the Trinity, as evidenced by the fact that everyone seems to be able to access this doctrine selectively in the interest of contradictory understandings of gender. In short, this entire line of theological reasoning is unhelpful and therefore neither an obstacle nor a boon to an investigation of gender.

2. For those readers interested in technical theology, yes, I am implying my agreement with the Western church in the matter of the *filioque* clause of the creed. But in this particular instance, I do not see how an Eastern reading would change things. In particular, celebrating *perichoresis* (the "dance" of the three members of the Trinity as it appears particularly in the Cappadocians) simply begs the question of hierarchy: Kings can dance with members of the royal family without anyone forgetting who is who. We might note also that the strongly patriarchal churches of the East clearly have no trouble endorsing sacred hierarchies of several sorts.

3. Capitalizing on feminine grammatical forms and feminine stereotypes of the Holy Spirit to characterize the Spirit in female terms—as even some evangelical Christians have been tempted to do—hardly helps the feminist cause: To do so still puts the female in the minority position (two "males" to one "female" in the Godhead) and, indeed, the subservient one.

*The submission of wives to husbands and the care of husbands
for wives provide an important picture of the relationship between
God and Israel and, later, between Christ and the church.*

There can be no disputing this basic observation of the way
God depicted his relationship with his people in the Bible. God
wonderfully took up the best traits of masculinity in ancient
cultures to tell believers important things about his love, power,
initiative, and faithfulness on their behalf.[4] He also modeled for
them, thereby, how husbands were to treat their wives in such
cultures—as Paul argues at some length in Ephesians 5 regarding
Christ and the church.[5]

Yet as we discussed earlier, a problem remains for those of
us in modern society in which the symbols have changed their
meanings. When patriarchy is odious and retains few of the posi-
tive connotations of its ancient heritage on which the biblical
portraits depend, and when women and men are equal so that

4. I discuss this point further in appendix B.
5. C. S. Lewis is among the many authors who celebrate this hierarchy, albeit
with his customary alertness to the limitation of all symbols. See his "Priestesses
in the Church?" in *God in the Dock: Essays on Theology and Ethics,* ed. Walter
Hooper (Grand Rapids: Eerdmans, 1970), 234–39. Lewis is now notorious for his
gendered language about a variety of theological points, including major ones.
For example, in *The Problem of Pain,* he suggests that "we are only creatures: our
rôle must always be that of patient to agent, female to male, mirror to light, echo
to voice. Our highest activity must be response, not initiative." In this popular
work, he also commends Christianity in language that is almost impossible for
a Christian feminist to stomach: Christianity itself, he says, has "the master
touch—the rough, male taste of reality, not made by us, or, indeed, for us, but
hitting us in the face" ([New York: Collier Books, 1962], 51, 25).
It is not my purpose here to "rescue" Lewis, hero of mine that he is. But it is
fascinating to read a much later work on the same subject, namely, the problem
of evil, in which he offers quite different-sounding reflections following his happy
marriage to Joy Davidman and his devastation at her death: "There is, hidden or
flaunted, a sword between the sexes till an entire marriage reconciles them. It
is arrogance in us to call frankness, fairness and chivalry 'masculine' when we
see them in a woman; it is arrogance in them, to describe a man's sensitiveness
or tact or tenderness as 'feminine.' But also what poor warped fragments of
humanity most mere men and mere women must be to make the implications
of that arrogance plausible. Marriage heals this. Jointly the two become fully
human. 'In the image of God created He *them.*' Thus, by a paradox, this carnival
of sexuality leads us out beyond our sexes" (*A Grief Observed* [New York: Bantam
Books, 1961], 57–58).

we no longer reflect anything of the vast difference between God and his people that previously was reflected by patriarchal marriage, does it make sense to carry on this symbolism? I doubt that God wants us to continue in what is now a deeply problematic drama, a drama that to many people today—both within the church and without—bespeaks a deity's domination of his inferiors rather than the intended message of our gracious Lord's care for his dependents.

So let us be clear: By maintaining egalitarianism in our place and time, we are not discarding these inspiring pictures of God's care for his people. We retain them in the Bible, embedded as they are in patriarchal cultures in which they made good sense. We can retrieve them from the Bible for our edification even in an egalitarian culture, as long as we do so with hermeneutical sensitivity to what God is and is not saying in such a depiction of himself and his beloved.[6]

The pastor is a priest, an intermediary between God and his people. Thus, he stands in for Christ, and only a male person can properly represent Christ in this role.

Roman Catholics have argued this way for a long time, given their particular sacramental understanding of priesthood. As a Protestant, however, I do not share this vision of what it means to pastor a church, and I defend the Protestant affirmation of the priesthood of all believers—not just clergy and not just males. Furthermore, I find it extremely odd that any other Protestant would take it seriously, as some apparently do.[7]

Were I persuaded, however, of this view of pastor as priest in the role of intermediary, I *still* would not find this argument compelling, for why is it Jesus Christ's maleness that must be figured in the person of the priest? Why not his Jewishness (so much for Gentiles), or his singleness (I realize that this is exactly the Roman Catholic argument for clerical celibacy), or

---

6. Again, see appendix B on this point.

7. It is perhaps not surprising that C. S. Lewis argues this way, given his Catholic leanings (see "Priestesses in the Church?"). It is more surprising to see it argued by that latter-day Puritan (and I use this term as both an objective description and a compliment!) J. I. Packer. See his "Let's Stop Making Women Presbyters," *Christianity Today* 35 (February 11, 1991): 18–21.

his middle-agedness (no younger or older priests, please), or his able-bodiedness (no room here for disabled people), and so on? The strongest point that can be made for the significance of the maleness of Jesus and therefore of priests is much like the previous argument: Maleness in a patriarchal culture bespeaks something important about God and God's representatives. But what about in an egalitarian situation? If the symbol no longer works, it seems not only pointless but also needlessly scandalous to retain it. Because I do not understand the pastoral ministry in the sense of a pastor functioning as an intermediary, I may well be missing something important here. Still, this argument strikes me as pointless even within the circles that do see pastors in this role. It certainly has no purchase on Protestants who do not.

So far, I have discussed the version of this argument in its explicit, "Catholic" sense. But I perceive that many Protestants who would never assert this kind of argument nonetheless believe in a surreptitious version of it. This version presumes that since the pastor is the head of the local church, as such Christians view ecclesiology, then such a person needs to be male, because only males are to lead.

A feminist critique of this view of church leadership, however, would suggest that women can lead as well as men can, and therefore there is no reason to forbid female clergy. A feminist critique, moreover, would go on to look at the structure of leadership itself and wonder, Why is there this hierarchy of One Big Boss? Why not, instead, a council or a college of pastors (whether employed full-time or part-time or volunteering as they can), each playing different and complementary roles? Wouldn't such a group of pastors best include both men and women, bringing their individual gifts and whatever also inheres in their maleness or femaleness, or masculinity or femininity, to the joint work of shepherding?

I put things this way because I am appealing to the broadest possible audience, and I do not feel I have to take sides in long-standing and complicated arguments about "sex versus gender" or "male/female essence versus the social construction of masculine or feminine identity." These matters are important, to be sure.[8] But I suggest that *whatever* one's views about them, it simply makes more biblical, theological, and pastoral sense not to put a solitary person on a pastoral pedestal.[9] It makes sense instead to entrust pastoral leadership to a group. Unless we construe leadership in strictly masculine terms—as some, alas, still do—then no matter what we make of male/female or masculine/feminine differences, we would want the richest possible array of relevant abilities in our pastoral team.[10]

Arguments from Church History

History shows us women in leadership only in pathological situations: extreme revivalism, schismatic groups, and the rise of cults.

We properly revere the early church fathers for bequeathing us much classic wisdom. But their general misogyny is a scandal: Most of them, as far as we know, really did see women as not only spiritually and intellectually inferior to men but also positively dangerous to men's godliness.

Such views are not confined, however, to late antiquity. Indeed, they remain to this day among some Christians who therefore espouse patriarchy as not only divinely ordained but also simply prudent, given women's clear inadequacies and vulnerabilities.[11]

8. For a useful summary of these issues from a Christian perspective, see Elaine Storkey, *Origins of Difference: The Gender Debate Revisited* (Grand Rapids: Baker Academic, 2001). See also Craig M. Gay, "'Gender' and the Idea of the Social Construction of Reality," in *Christian Perspectives on Gender, Sexuality, and Community,* ed. Maxine Hancock, 167–80 (Vancouver, BC: Regent College Publishing, 2003).

9. I argue this point at length in "A Double Copernican Revolution: Leadership and Membership in the Church," in John G. Stackhouse, Jr., *Evangelical Landscapes: Facing Critical Issues of the Day* (Grand Rapids: Baker Academic, 2002), 37–45. See also the conclusions in Stanley J. Grenz, with Denise Muir Kjesbo, *Women in the Church: A Biblical Theology of Women in Ministry* (Downers Grove, IL: InterVarsity, 1995).

10. David Basinger submits this line of thinking to searching philosophical critique in "Gender Roles, Scripture, and Science: Some Clarifications," *Christian Scholar's Review* 17 (March 1988): 241–53.

11. See appendix B in William J. Webb, *Slaves, Women, and Homosexuals* (Downers Grove, IL: InterVarsity, 2001), 263–68, for a shockingly wide sample from the history of the church. See Webb's appendix C (269–73) for a brief

A classic instance of this sort of argument appears in a text-book widely used among evangelicals:

> The history of Theosophy then, is marked indelibly by the imprint of the female minds [sic], which, ever since Eve, has apparently been vulnerable to forbidden fruit and the tantalizing tones of various varieties of serpents.
>
> It should be remembered that the Apostle Paul strictly enjoined the Christian Church to forbid women the teaching ministry, especially when men were available to meet this need . . . (1 Timothy 2:11–14).
>
> It can be clearly seen from the study of non-Christian cults, ancient and modern, that the female teaching ministry has graphically fulfilled what Paul anticipated in his day by divine revelation, and brought in its wake, as history tells us, confusion, division and strife. This is true from Johanna Southcutt to Mary Baker Eddy to Helena Blavatsky and the Fox sisters, all of whom were living proof of our Lord's declaration that "if the blind lead the blind, both shall fall into the ditch" (Matthew 15:14b).[12]

The immediate response to this nonsense is simple: If it is true that a few cults have been founded by women, then we might well ask, Who began all the other cults—that is, the vast majority of them? That's right. It was non-women. (And, we might add, who has been responsible for the vast majority of heresies as well as the mass of deficient theology taught throughout the ages within the church? It is the same group, and it is not women.) Mercifully, no responsible complementarians argue this way anymore.

From the other side of the debate comes the recognition of women in leadership that was indeed on the margins: the Montanist movement; various women's orders in the Middle Ages, perhaps most notably the Beguines; the notorious case of Anne

---

survey of social scientific studies of whether women are, in fact, more prone to deception than men. (Conclusion: They aren't.)

12. Walter R. Martin, *The Kingdom of the Cults: An Analysis of the Major Cult Systems in the Present Christian Era* (1965; repr., Minneapolis: Bethany, 1974), 225. More than one person has observed that Genesis 3 actually gives the intellectual nod to Eve, who at least seemed to consider the question of eating the forbidden fruit, while Adam simply took what his wife gave him and ate it.

Hutchinson in Puritan New England; female preachers in the eighteenth- and nineteenth-century revivals; and the prominent place of women among Pentecostal and charismatic clergy in the twentieth and twenty-first centuries.

For some traditional Christians, this checkered heritage proves that women are not to lead in mainstream churches. There is, however, a transparent circularity to this logic. If women have not been allowed to lead within mainstream Christianity but only in the occasional marginal movement, then female leadership necessarily is linked with marginal movements—thus disqualifying it from mainstream consideration!

What is perhaps more positively suggestive is the presence of female leadership even within mainstream movements of various sorts: female abbesses, mystics, and teachers in the Middle Ages, such as Margery Kempe, Julian of Norwich, and Hildegard of Bingen;[13] female evangelists and preachers encouraged by Charles Finney in the United States and by the Salvation Army in the United Kingdom and then worldwide; female pastors trained by such mainstream institutions as Moody Bible Institute at the turn of the twentieth century (even as that institution turned against the idea of women in pastoral leadership in later decades);[14] female missionaries and parachurch leaders from all denominations throughout the great century of Protestant missions and beyond;[15] and women speakers today who command considerable audiences as Bible teachers and authors even as their message is ostensibly a traditional, complementarist one,

13. Patricia Hampl makes an intriguing point: "What is often overlooked, especially in recent times, about the Catholic tradition: in spite of its glaring refusals and inequities regarding women, it remains the only Western tradition that has an unbroken history of providing a respected way of life for women outside the domestic role of wife-and-mother. The work of a nun and of a monk is identical: the *Opus Dei*, the work of God—to pray. Specifically, to pray without ceasing" ("Edith Stein," in *Martyrs: Contemporary Writers on Modern Lives of Faith*, ed. Susan Bergman [Maryknoll, NY: Orbis, 1996], 206).

14. Janette Hassey, *No Time for Silence: Evangelical Women in Public Ministry around the Turn of the Century* (Grand Rapids: Zondervan, 1986).

15. R. Pierce Beaver, *American Protestant Women in World Mission: History of the First Feminist Movement in North America*, rev. ed. (1968; repr., Grand Rapids: Eerdmans, 1980).

such as Elisabeth Elliot and Anne Graham Lotz. These examples cannot be dismissed as marginal.

Nowadays, of course, we also can consider the experience of mainstream Protestant churches throughout the West that have employed women in pastoral and theological leadership for decades. Will anyone seriously gainsay the effectiveness of their labors? What, indeed, can complementarians make of the evident fruitfulness of their ministries among white, black, Hispanic, and other congregations in North America, the U.K., Europe, Australia, New Zealand, and elsewhere? The best answer is that God still prefers only men to do it but will settle for the work being done by whoever will do it. This answer does not satisfy me.

Instead, one might conclude that the paradigm I am offering does a better job of explaining the data: God goes along with the general social contours of patriarchal society, even as the impress of the Holy Spirit on that society first ameliorates some of the most oppressive aspects of patriarchy and then ultimately opens it up to the full equality of women. The church, especially when it is in the white heat of revival, shows us glimpses of the order of the kingdom of God to come, but the world is not ready for it yet, so the movements subside into patriarchy, awaiting the day when such compromise is no longer strategic. That day has come in some societies. (Again, I am not arguing that the day of the Lord has come but rather that the opportunity for Christian egalitarianism has arisen in the context of the broader social reality of egalitarianism in modern societies.) Therefore, the mainstreaming of women's full dignity in home and church should be a priority for all Christians in such cultures.

Christian feminism is simply a capitulation to secular feminism. It is a case of sheer worldliness.

The contention of some complementarians that Christian feminists are a pathetic group of wannabes chasing after the bandwagon of secular feminism, desperate to be *au courant* and politically correct, can be answered in two ways.[16]

---

16. A popular presentation of this contention can be found in Mary A. Kassian, *The Feminist Gospel: The Movement to Unite Feminism with the Church* (Wheaton: Crossway, 1992). For important perspectives on the fear of feminism among

First, the charge is not true. Christian feminism is a hundred years older than the books of Betty Friedan and Gloria Steinem on this side of the Atlantic and of Simone de Beauvoir on the other. Christian feminism arose in the nineteenth century in temperance movements, suffragist movements, and in America in particular alongside abolitionist movements. Therefore, if the *post hoc ergo propter hoc* (after this, therefore because of it) fallacy is to be maintained, one ought to argue (implausibly, to be sure) that Ms. Friedan and others are the ones who are trying to catch up.[17]

The second response to the charge that Christian feminism is merely a response to secular feminism is that even if it were true, it would not necessarily be a bad thing. Who cares where a good idea comes from first? In the providence of God, feminist values of human dignity and human rights have come to be championed by secularists, Jews, and others. Christians properly recognize and rejoice in these truths, even if we are slower than some others to grasp them.

In fact, however, we recognize that these values clearly emerged out of the particular matrix of Western civilization that was shaped so deeply by biblical religion—and only in that matrix. Instead of resisting these values, therefore, we can be humbly grateful for this provocation from some non-Christians, as well as our fellow Christians, to recover forgotten aspects of our own tradition.

As Dietrich Bonhoeffer tirelessly reminded us, Christ is the Lord of the whole world, not just of the church, and he is at work by the Spirit in the whole world, not just in the church.[18]

---

conservative evangelicals, see Betty A. DeBerg, *Ungodly Women: Gender and the First Wave of American Fundamentalism* (Minneapolis: Fortress, 1990); Sally K. Gallagher, *Evangelical Identity and Gendered Family Life* (New Brunswick: Rutgers University Press, 2003); and Julie Ingersoll, *Evangelical Christian Women: War Stories in the Gender Battles* (New York: New York University Press, 2003).

17. Of course, no one does argue that, partly because Christian feminism in several quarters fell on hard times in the first half of the twentieth century, and partly because any sort of traditional Christianity was invisible in the social and mental worlds of the secular feminists of the 1950s and beyond.

18. Bonhoeffer elaborates on this theme in his *Ethics*: "There are not two realities, but only one reality, and that is the reality of God, which has become manifest in Christ in the reality of the world. . . . The world is not divided

If someone is willing to protect the weak, feed the hungry, free the oppressed, beautify the land, or teach the truth, Christians properly give thanks to the one true God from whom all blessings flow. Thus, Christian feminists can celebrate any sort of feminism that brings more justice and human flourishing to the world—more shalom—no matter who is bringing it, since we recognize the hand of God in all that is good.[19] As Stephen Carter remarks, "Religious conservatives who rail against feminism would do well to consider the centuries of male non-integrity that gave feminism birth."[20] We Christians then can contribute to feminism the distinctive insights of the gospel and especially the model of our Lord Jesus, who shows us God's will toward women and men better than does anyone else.

Arguments from Contemporary Experience and Practice

This kind of argument can be used to support the legitimization of homosexuality.

It is true that certain kinds of feminist arguments can be deployed in the service of defending homosexuality as a valid form of human love. I do not agree, however, that the paradigm I have offered can be used in this campaign. In short, the cases are not parallel.

To be sure, inasmuch as homosexuals have been treated politically as subhuman, Christians must fight for their fundamental human rights as hard as for anyone else's. Homosexuals are our neighbors—indeed, some of them are our fellow Christians—and we must love them as we love ourselves. Yet one of the key debating points in this larger public question is just what con-

---

between Christ and the devil, but, whether it recognizes it or not, it is solely and entirely the world of Christ. . . . Any static delimitation of a region which belongs to the devil and a region which belongs to Christ is a denial of the reality of God's having reconciled the whole world with Himself in Christ" (Dietrich Bonhoeffer, *Ethics*, trans. Neville Horton Smith [1955; repr., New York: Simon & Schuster/Touchstone, 1995], 195, 201–2).

19. Richard J. Mouw, *He Shines in All That's Fair: Culture and Common Grace* (Grand Rapids: Eerdmans, 2001).

20. Stephen L. Carter, *Integrity* (New York: Basic Books, 1996), 151.

stitutes a human right and what constitutes social privileges, responsibilities, and so on. Robert Benne and Gerald McDermott illustrate this point in regard to the controversy over homosexual marriage:

> There are huge differences between constitutional rights with few restrictions (such as the rights to life or free speech) and other rights with important restrictions, which do not carry the right of universal access. We already recognize that not everyone has the right to enlist in the army, but that one must be of the proper age, physical condition, citizenship, and philosophy—anarchists and pacifists need not apply. We also agree that certain persons do not have the right to marriage—children, multiple partners, family members, and those already married.[21]

Christians, therefore, must continue to work for full justice for all, including our homosexual neighbors, while recognizing that the debate is not over as to what "full justice" means for homosexuals—and for everyone else.

Even if one were to argue, however, that the full legitimization of homosexuality is indeed a political issue that is parallel to racism and sexism, there is still no comfort to be found in my paradigm. I am convinced that while there is significant tension in the Bible regarding slavery (on the one hand, slaves and masters are equal before God; on the other hand, slavery is at least temporarily condoned) and gender (again, on the one hand, women and men are equal and equally gifted before God; on the other hand, patriarchy is at least temporarily condoned), there is no such tension regarding homosexuality. The Bible presents a pattern that supports both the temporary, culture-specific accommodation of slavery and patriarchy and also the principles that not only support but also compel the causes of abolitionism and feminism. There is no such double pattern regarding homosexuality.

The Bible instead is univocal, from cover to cover, on the matter of sexual intercourse: The only legitimate and healthy pattern is heterosexual, adult, and exclusive within the covenant

---

21. Robert Benne and Gerald McDermott, "Thirteen Bad Arguments for Same-Sex Marriage," *Christianity Today* 48 (September 2004): 51.

of marriage. Not only is homosexuality ruled out, but so is every other form of sexuality that is not oriented toward and consummated within the lifelong marriage of a man and a woman.

Indeed, resistance to the religious redefinition of marriage to include same-sex unions is a matter on which egalitarians and complementarians can and should agree.[22] Christians recognize that from Genesis 2 onward the Bible assumes that there is something crucially complementary about the marriage of a man and a woman (versus *same*-sex unions), just as God created humanity in his image as male and female in Genesis 1. Current wisdom cannot define precisely and to everyone's satisfaction in what that complementarity consists. No "essential" definition of man and woman commands the field, while many fear any such "essentialism" entirely as a tool for the continuing denigration of women and confinement of them in predetermined roles.[23] But the biblical pattern implies that there *is* something crucially complementary to this union of one man and one woman that no other form of union (not polygamy or polyandry, not homosexuality, not serial marriages) can represent properly and thus constitute a proper marriage.

More particularly, the biblical proscription of homosexuality is not arbitrary. The Bible presents homosexuality as a psychospiritual pathology, whether it results from nature, nurture, personal choice, or a combination of these. Debates about its origin possibly can be helpful in terms of awareness, therapy, and mutual understanding and respect, but they are also impor-

22. Whether Christians should urge secular, pluralistic states to recognize or to resist civil same-sex marriage is more a question of political strategy. I believe Christians can disagree with one another in good conscience as to whether the gospel will be furthered more by one strategy or another. There are gains and losses either way: A Christian view of marriage might prevail in a campaign for traditional marriage, but in such a controversy, Christians may also come to be seen increasingly as both generally imperialistic and particularly homophobic. Thus, even some moderate people will become hardened against our gospel proclamation.

23. A helpful survey of recent research is offered in Storkey, *Origins of Difference*, 76–86. Mary Stewart Van Leeuwen provides an extended discussion of the question of male/female similarities and differences in *Gender and Grace: Love, Work, and Parenting in a Changing World* (Downers Grove, IL: InterVarsity, 1990).

tantly beside the point here. So what if people do not choose to be homosexual, as I doubt anyone does? The origin of *anyone's* personal deformation—whether pride, alcoholism, promiscuity, self-loathing, self-righteousness, or violence—is not the issue in the Bible so much as is the proper *response* to it.[24] Homosexuality therefore incurs certain restrictions appropriate to its character, such as celibacy, just as the promiscuous must be chaste, the pedophiliac must avoid children, and the self-righteous must seek humility.[25]

Contrarily, one's being female or being a member of an oppressed people is not itself bad: Indeed, the evil consists instead in the condition of subjugation by patriarchy or slavery when nothing about one's nature justifies such treatment.

This small book is not about homosexuality, so I cannot and should not try to develop a full discussion of it here. I simply indicate why there is no important parallel between the cause of feminism and the cause of homosexual legitimization.[26]

Now, the two arguments that give me the most pause do not stem from biblical, theological, or historical grounds. I'm reason-

24. I recognize that in many instances homosexuality might not be cured in this life, just as other psychospiritual pathologies might not be (such as personality disorders, which incidentally mark many prominent clergy and theologians, among others). On some of the larger questions here, see Thomas Schmidt, *Straight and Narrow: Compassion and Clarity in the Homosexuality Debate* (Downers Grove, IL: InterVarsity, 1995); and Stanley J. Grenz, *Welcoming but Not Affirming: An Evangelical Response to Homosexuality* (Philadelphia: Westminster John Knox, 1998).

25. I acknowledge that in this deeply troubled world some people will find the first serious and genuine love of their lives in a homosexual relationship. I believe therefore that such relationships can be condoned, cautiously, for pastoral, therapeutic reasons as temporary accommodations to some people's particular injuries and needs. The church nonetheless does not "bless" such unions, let alone "normalize" them, but upholds scriptural sexual and relational ethics as the ideal toward which we all strive. In the meanwhile, however, we can appreciate the sad truth that some people will have to take the long way home, and a caring homosexual relationship may be a necessary part of that journey. This is clearly a difficult area of pastoral ethics and requires deep theological, psychological, and spiritual wisdom.

26. See Webb, *Slaves, Women, and Homosexuals,* for a sustained examination of the case of homosexuality alongside the questions of slavery and patriarchy.

ably satisfied on those grounds with the model I have presented as the best of those I have encountered so far. But I do want to heed two warnings, the first from complementarians and the second from feminists, that challenge the practical implications of this model.

If women do not stay home, children will be neglected.

In early 2004, the *Atlantic* magazine featured a cover story on how white, middle-class feminist women have been able to realize their dream of entering the workplace while also having children. They have done so, the article suggests, only by hiring other women to care for those children and to help with the housework—the female share of which has not diminished in many households, despite protestations from men about how enlightened they are about feminism. Indeed, as one wag has put it, "Feminism means that women now have to look after the car too." The Supermom cannot do it all or have it all. So in this scenario, children are not neglected, but they are being raised by caregivers who are not their parents.[27]

Further down the economic ladder, however, are many working mothers who are not realizing a "dream" but are working because they have to. Either they are single—as many mothers are in North America—or the cost of living is such that they must join their husbands in the workforce. Their children have to be placed in a day care that is often of dubious quality. Thus, there is a weird handing-over of children from richer to poorer down a chain of wealth.

Caring for children while staying afloat economically is a genuine challenge for most and a dreadful one for many. Simply preaching a return to the "traditional family" is no answer. This sort of family is not found in the Bible or in most of the history of the church. It is instead the family typical of a particular era: the post–World War II boom in which Dad could earn a household's worth of income even on an assembly line while everyone else could stay home or in school. Such a family now has largely vanished from the economic landscape.

27. Caitlin Flanagan, "How Serfdom Saved the Women's Movement," *Atlantic* 293 (March 2004): 109–28.

Many argue that these wages have disappeared because women have entered the workforce, and thus employers can lower wages in the face of a greater supply of workers. Thus, feminism is to blame. I am no economist, but obviously there are other factors at stake, such as increased mechanization facilitated by computers that has replaced many industrial and clerical jobs. Globalization, facilitated by lower-cost long-distance transportation, changed tariffs, and improved telecommunications, has resulted in many jobs being moved "offshore." (The latter development is one that North American Christians should be careful about condemning, since it has brought a measure of wealth to formerly impoverished regions elsewhere.)

Wherever the blame lies—if "blame" is even a useful concept in matters of economic and social evolution—the traditionalist attempt to turn back the clock will not help. There is no point in calling everyone to move back to Levittown and *Leave It to Beaver*. It is simply absurd, as well as offensive, to suggest that these various and complex social ills would be cured if we would just put men back in charge.

Feminism can help here by reframing the challenge for each family: Instead of "women's work" or "men's work," there is just *work*, and *we* have to get it done somehow. So what are *we* going to do? If it turns out that many more women than men prefer to tend the home and care for the children most of the time—whether from nature or nurture (who knows?)—then so be it. Those families are choosing together what to do, not automatically relegating the woman to the domestic sphere and the man to the marketplace. Those unusual families in which the woman goes out to work and the man stays home (I have one set of relatives who have followed this pattern at times, and our youngest son has had excellent before- and after-school care from a man in a family such as this) are also free to practice this pattern without emasculating the man or defeminizing the woman. An intermediate arrangement, such as many families now practice (one or both spouses working less than full-time and sharing in various domestic duties), also enjoys the same legitimacy. The liberty here is to do whatever makes the most of the particular gifts, desires, opportunities, and needs of the individuals who make up a particular family, without simplistically sorting things according to sex.

Does anyone still want to argue seriously that all mothers, everywhere and always, are much more suited to domestic duties, and all men, everywhere and always, are much more suited to the workplace? Again, social science demonstrates what we all now know from our own experience: Such universal generalizations just are not true of every couple. Therefore, we need a paradigm that includes and guides everyone, not just most.[28]

If this paradigm is to be believed, then the church should not only tolerate but also comply with patriarchy today in the many parts of the world that still practice it—and that seems repugnant.

One critical *feminist* response to the paradigm I present in this book is that this proposal is tolerant of the oppression of women and therefore tolerant of sin. Indeed, this paradigm encourages Christians to perpetuate patriarchal structures in those parts of the world in which society is not prepared to embrace full equality for women. Even worse, from a feminist point of view, is the sin of ascribing such tolerance of patriarchy to the will of God, as if the Holy One can not only look upon sin but also put up with it indefinitely, and even work through it.

This charge is one I take seriously. As a feminist and an egalitarian (albeit a white, privileged, male feminist and egalitarian), I dislike the notion of contributing the slightest legitimacy to the perpetuation of patriarchy. As a Christian, furthermore, I *hate* the notion that I would ascribe to God something unworthy of him—indeed, something evil.

As I look hard at the Bible, however, and at the two thousand years of church history since the Bible's completion, it seems evident that God has accommodated himself over and over to the weakness and even the sin of human beings. He also has called his faithful ones to a similar accommodation. The "already but not yet" tension is clear not only with the coming of Christ but also throughout the Old Testament story of redemption. God chooses a people as a vehicle for global

---

28. See Storkey, *Origins of Difference*; and Van Leeuwen, *Gender and Grace*.

salvation and then works with them in a convoluted trajectory of obedience and blessing, disobedience and punishment, first this way and then that way. God puts up with a compromised plan for the conquest of Canaan, blesses a monarchy he did not want, forestalls the prophesied judgment on both northern and southern kingdoms for generations, and even then preserves a remnant and reestablishes it in Jerusalem. God works not only through Israel but also through the empires of Egypt, Assyria, Babylon, Persia, and Rome. God works not only through prophets and saints but also through Joseph's brothers, Balaam and his donkey, Nebuchadnezzar and Darius, Caiaphas and Pilate.

Much more needs to be said on this matter.[29] It remains evident in Scripture and history, however, that God "draws straight with crooked lines" on the tortured topography of the troubled creation he loves and is redeeming. He calls us to do the same.

Yet this paradigm should not be construed as a call to acquiesce to patriarchy. Much less is it a blessing upon it. Patriarchy is a result of the fall. As Cornelius Plantinga suggests about sin in general, patriarchy particularly is "not the way it's supposed to be."[30] Instead, the paradigm offered here echoes the fundamental biblical call to work for shalom, for the full flourishing of every woman and every man, every slave and every master, every child and every parent, as God gives us opportunity to do so.

Where and when God does not give us opportunity to do so, however, we pray that he will soon. And in the meanwhile—that is a crucial phrase in this paradigm, *in the meanwhile*—we trust him to work his good will in and through us, whatever the structures with which we temporarily must comply. Thus, we will indeed have to comply with patriarchy, with corrupt gov-

---

29. I have said more in my book on the problem of evil (*Can God Be Trusted? Faith and the Challenge of Evil* [New York: Oxford University Press, 1998]), and I hope to say still more in my next book on a theology of culture.

30. Plantinga, quoting a line from the film *Grand Canyon* as the title of his book, *Not the Way It's Supposed to Be: A Breviary of Sin* (Grand Rapids: Eerdmans, 1995).

ernments, with exploitative businesses, and with hypocritical charities, for where will we find wholly pure institutions and societies, the ones not deeply touched by evil in this world? *In the meanwhile*, we live as the patriarchs lived, as the prophets lived, as the apostles lived, and as the saints—women and men—in every age have lived. We live with hope in God that one day all this tension, compromise, and accommodation to our sin will be done away. We live with the sure sense that God is right here with us, comforting us in our oppression, forgiving us our sins—even sins of complicity with evil—grieving with us that things have to be this way for now, and empowering us nonetheless to bring gospel light to the darkest corners of the earth.

I find it difficult to advance this idea. I am sure it was much more difficult for dedicated Christian feminist Gretchen Gaebelein Hull to make this same point almost twenty years ago when she addressed to her sisters in Christ the following poignant plea:

> Can *you* drink the cup of submission? Yes, I realize full well what many of you are thinking: *That's all we've ever done.* But I would ask of you: Can you now drink the cup as Christ means you to drink it? Not because you must, but because you choose to? Would you be willing to put aside your legitimate rights, if the time to exercise them is not yet right in your particular circumstances? Would you be willing to put your career on hold, if that is in the best interests of your family or your cultural milieu? Will you work for change in a patient and loving manner, rather than sinking into anger or bitterness? Will you commit yourself to work in a Christ-like way, even if you are in un-Christ-like situations?[31]

I perhaps can clarify this point by acknowledging that the argument I am setting out in this book would apply—in part—to the terribly vexing problem faced by Christians today in many parts of Africa, namely, polygamy. As thousands, even millions, convert to Christianity, Christian leaders properly call them to

31. Gretchen Gaebelein Hull, *Equal to Serve: Women and Men in the Church and Home* (Old Tappan, NJ: Revell, 1987), 241.

Christian morality, which includes Christian marriage of just one man and one woman. In many of the social contexts in which these converts must continue to live, however, for a man to set aside every wife but his first and all children from subsequent marriages would be to surrender them to disaster. Women have so little opportunity to make a living on their own—beyond prostitution and other horrific occupations—that Christian leaders feel caught in a clash of Christian values.

Applying my paradigm to this situation would involve recognizing polygamy—as it appears in the Old Testament just as it appears today in Africa—as an accommodation to deep social problems, and as itself a social problem, not as God's ideal. (One struggles in vain to find a happy polygamous home anywhere in the Old Testament.) Thus, Christian leaders have condoned polygamy where it seems the most helpful way *for women and children*, the "little ones" and the oppressed in these social structures. As they do so, however, they simultaneously teach the better way of Christian monogamy and work for the transformation of society such that polygamy can be done away as soon as possible.

The parallel with my suggestion regarding patriarchy is only partial, however, for polygamy can be seen as the best of available options for the women themselves in certain societies. So why should we tolerate patriarchy when it is *not* the best option for women? We should do so only because the only other course—resistance to patriarchy—would somehow harm the cause of the gospel, perhaps by embittering people against Christianity, and has little or no prospect of actually helping change the status of women (as was the case in first-century churches). This attitude, then, represents a form of Christian realism that seeks the advance of the gospel above all other values with a clear-eyed recognition of what can and cannot be done in a given situation. Thus (and I say this carefully), polygamy itself would be tolerated even if it were *not* better for women—as slavery certainly was not better for slaves—if higher gospel priorities were at stake.[32]

32. The history of missions must not be whitewashed. It is replete with examples of tensions such as these that strain Christian fidelity to the point that

This is a hard saying indeed. But compliance with patriarchy ought to be undertaken only with grief over its evil and with a determination to ameliorate it as quickly and as extensively as possible. Furthermore, we Christians must keep the pressure on our society to keep changing its ways for the better in terms of gender as on all other fronts of shalom-making—including pressing our own families and churches to change.

For once in this book I write as a man to men: We still have more power than women, and we must seek to use it on their behalf in a way that is appropriate to our particular context. In most cases in North American society today, that context means that men must join women in the vanguard of Christian feminism in our homes, churches, and beyond. This is our opportunity to advocate for the other. This is what it means to love our women as we love ourselves.

To be sure, we Christians are not God's only agents of change, neither as individuals nor as the church. We must beware Christian talk that suggests we *are* God's only agent of change—as if nothing will happen if we do not do it. God is himself the primary agent of all good change, and he works through all the means available to him, including individuals and institutions that do not praise him and yet must accomplish his providential will. Both the Bible and world history show us that God works in mysterious ways and through many unexpected channels to achieve his purposes.

Let us do our part, then, with vigor, creativity, perseverance, hope, and humility before the sovereign agenda of God. Let us press against sin of every kind to see whether a God-given op-

---

some values are sacrificed—for better or for worse—for the sake of others. Philip Jenkins points to the seventeenth-century Jesuit Robert De Nobili, a hero of Roman Catholic missions, who posed as a Hindu guru, adopted the local dress, and—in what was clearly scandalous according to Christian ethics in general but was done precisely to avoid scandal in that missionary situation—observed the caste system, such that he refused to treat the poor on equal terms. Jenkins frankly acknowledges this contradiction of the teachings of Jesus and yet concludes, "This represented a successful missionary strategy, and perhaps the only one that could have worked in the setting of the time" (Philip Jenkins, *The Next Christendom: The Coming of Global Christianity* [New York: Oxford University Press, 2002], 30).

portunity is there to increase shalom.[33] But where it is evidently not time for this idea or practice to yield, we must not resort to revolutionary violence that will impede a society's reception of the gospel without yielding actual benefit for the oppressed. This principle can also apply to small societies such as individual families and congregations. Again, if the family or church in question is not ripe for change, forcing the issue will result only in damage to the measure of shalom already achieved in that society.

Some will feel they must leave such recalcitrant churches for freer ministry elsewhere, but many of us cannot, or ought not, leave such churches, nor can we leave our families or national societies. If we stay, we ought to promote gospel priorities as best we can, stay alert for any new openings, and yearn for the day when all such compromises will be rendered unnecessary.

What, Then, Are We to Do?

As we seek to respond properly to a social situation involving patriarchy—whether a marriage or a church, in the instances discussed in this book—there are a number of principles that can guide us. Some of these principles are as follows: activism, realism, vocation, and hope.

Activism. "Blessed are the peacemakers," preached Jesus, and we should make all the shalom we can. In particular, we

---

33. I commend the concept of "hesitation" as articulated in Glenn Tinder's highly suggestive book, *The Political Meaning of Christianity*: "The prophetic stance is an ideal of taking full cognizance of our common worldly circumstances, being mindful of both our limitations and our responsibilities, and in that frame of mind waiting for God.

"We recognize the priority of waiting when we hesitate before acting. We thus take time to remember our finitude and sinfulness and to remind ourselves that the initiative does not belong to human beings. Hesitation is a formality required of us when we cross the frontier between waiting and action; it is also a formality that in the midst of action we occasionally pause and repeat. Like all significant formalities, it is a mark of respect—for God and the creatures with whom we share the earth. And it expresses humility: there are values and realities beyond our understanding and control" ([Baton Rouge: Louisiana State University Press, 1989], 164).

should further the flourishing of human society by the fullest possible participation of women and men, without prejudice or constraint. We cannot perfect our marriages, churches, or larger societies, and we are not called to do so. We are called instead to do what we can to extend the kingdom of God. Therefore, if we can improve a marriage or a church, we should, as part of our participation in kingdom living.

Realism. Jesus told us to love God and to love our neighbors. But we need to see as clearly as we can what it means to love God and our neighbors in a given situation. Given a particular set of circumstances, what does God want to have happen? Given the apparent limitations, what are God's priorities? Given who the neighbors are, in what ways can I love them, and in what ways will they let me do so? Such realism will help us make the necessary hard decisions in a world in which we typically cannot succeed in everything we attempt, a world in which we frequently have to settle for half a loaf, a world in which we often confront a conflict of values and have to work for the higher at the cost of the lower.

Vocation. God calls us all to come to Christ, to follow him, and to grow up to maturity in him. He calls the church to work with him in his great mission of drawing the world back to himself. He also calls us individually to a particular service, according to the gifts, limitations, and circumstances of our particular lives.

Hope. God gives us immediate hope that our current labor, however vexed by suffering, will produce lasting results as it is validated and assisted by him. God also gives us the great final hope that our suffering will cease, that injustice will be terminated, and that soon Christ will return to establish his kingdom of lasting shalom.

How, then, can these principles apply to particular sets of challenges and opportunities?

Fundamentally, we need to do what we can to improve our marriages and our churches. If nothing can be done right now, then we need to stay alert to what can be done tomorrow. In the meanwhile, we imitate the pattern of Jesus as best we can in all we do, especially in our domestic and ecclesial relationships. But usually something *can* be done now, and we are encouraged by God to do it. Some marriages and churches are ripe for change, and it is my hope that this book will encourage and facilitate such change.

We also need to consider, however, just what an individual or a particular group or class of people can accomplish in a given situation. Many young people, for example, will not be heard by the elders in a particular church, no matter how right they are. Many women will not be heard by many men. It is not fair, and it is not good, but it is the way it is. Such Christians need to decide among their *real* options how they can best honor God and advance his kingdom. As soon as possible, they should jettison any illusion that they will be heard simply on the merits of their arguments and regardless of the social realities of the situation.

Lest I be misheard on this point, let me affirm my belief that the Holy Spirit can transform hearts and does so sometimes in surprising ways. But we need to see realistically that what we are talking about now is a suspension of normal human relations, what I call a "sociological miracle." If we do not have strong grounds to expect such a miracle in a given instance, then we should make other choices—before we become bitter not only at our fellow church members for their recalcitrance but also at God for not performing the miracle we sought.

The principle of realism further reminds us that there are some situations in which pushing feminism too fast and too far will cause rupture and even destruction of a marriage or a congregation. That seems, at least generally, not to be God's will. The ideologue may draw personal satisfaction from his or her purity and zeal, but God cares about actual people much more than he does about abstract principles. He has shown himself willing to bring us along patiently, as fast as we can go, but only as fast as we can go. In some circumstances, therefore, the policy needs to be slow, steady pressure on a marriage or a church to change yet with appreciative support for all the genuine work the Spirit is doing therein.

It remains that perhaps, in a given church, it is best for those convinced of egalitarianism to take leave of those who are not so convinced. The result can be two churches of integrity rather than one that seethes with suspicion and resentment, to the cost of the kingdom of God. In the case of individual members who feel they are on the margins, the kingdom of God may well be better advanced by someone withdrawing from a given body and joining another church. Thus, the individual will not be impeded in his or her ministry, nor will either church be impeded in its own.

In the case of a marriage, divorce would be an option only if the patriarchal treatment of the wife is severe enough. What counts as "severe enough" would have to be assessed in context, of course. God loves us all and grieves over anyone's suffering. He also particularly cares for the vulnerable and the oppressed. But it remains true also that God sometimes calls us to difficult relationships, and we are not to leave just any unpleasant situation. This is genuine Christian liberty: to use our freedom for God, our neighbor, and ourselves.

Let me be clear. Someone suffering abuse should free herself or himself from it if she or he possibly can. It is a dreadful thing, and no proper Christian teaching about suffering in general, or about voluntary subordination within marriage or church, can bless abuse by telling people to stay in such situations if they can escape them. We especially must guard against the tolerance of abuse "for the sake of the church's reputation" or "for the sake of the pastor's reputation," for abuse happens in Christian and even clerical homes, and it must be rooted out there as it must be rooted out everywhere else.[34]

In a culture, however, in which many people leave churches and marriages as freely as they leave jobs and clubs when they encounter a little genuine hardship, or even mere disappointment, the ethical tension is inescapable. We can counsel neither "stick it out at all costs" nor "leave when you like." We must recall God's priorities and sort things through as carefully as we can, ideally with the help of Christian sisters and brothers who can share their wisdom and provide practical support.

34. Nancy Nason-Clark, *The Battered Wife: How Christians Confront Family Violence* (Louisville: Westminster John Knox, 1997); Catherine Clark Kroeger and Nancy Nason-Clark, *No Place for Abuse: Biblical and Practical Resources to Counteract Domestic Violence* (Downers Grove, IL: InterVarsity, 2001); and Nancy Nason-Clark and Catherine Clark Kroeger, *Refuge from Abuse: Healing and Hope for Abused Christian Women* (Downers Grove, IL: InterVarsity, 2004).

Finally, I want to affirm the principle of vocation in this sense: God calls different people to different kinds of activism. Some situations need firebrands to provoke the rest of us to the ideas and actions we ought to have thought and done on our own. Some situations need mediators to help make temperate and edifying communication possible. Some situations need friendly people who work hard at maintaining good relations across ideological divides. Some situations need patient people who go about their kingdom business and put up with whatever afflictions come their way.

These different sorts of people can annoy one another during a controversy. The activists cannot understand why the friendly people would fraternize with the enemy. The mediators wish the activists would stop setting fires for the mediators to put out. The patient people often do not see what all the fuss is about and sometimes question the motives and the usefulness of all this activity.

Let us appreciate that some situations need *all* these people at the *same* time, each contributing according to his or her gifts, limitations, and opportunities. Let us, each and all, seek how to love God and our neighbors as best we can while supporting other people following their callings in their own ways. This is how the kingdom of God has advanced, and will advance, to the final benefit of all women and men and to the glory of the God who loves us so much.

And Now, Your Turn . . .

Such conclusions cannot sit easily with any feminist, and I doubt that they satisfy any complementarian. But may I say again that the theological challenge is not to solve every difficulty perfectly. Nor is it to convince everyone. The theological challenge for me, and for you, and for all of us in our churches is to select the best option among those available. I believe this paradigm takes seriously the concerns, arguments, and strengths of both sides and also compensates for at least some of the weaknesses of both sides. It squares best with the eschatological tension in which we really live: "already but not yet." It matches up best with the pattern of God's actual activity in the Bible, as well as with particular teachings about gender. And it has been borne out in the history of the church.

I do not pretend, however, to have solved every exegetical, theological, historical, or practical problem even to my own satisfaction, much less to anyone else's. Thus, I recall Paul's good advice: "Each of us will be accountable to God. Let us therefore no longer pass judgment on one another, but resolve instead never to put a stumbling block or hindrance in the way of another" (Rom. 14:12–13).

I ask, then, that you will forgive me if any of this book has been a stumbling block or a hindrance to you. Set it aside if it has. There has been too much antagonism, even violence, in this debate. My prayer instead has been to follow the scriptural injunction, "Let us consider how to provoke one another to love and good deeds" (Heb. 10:24). If you have been provoked, I pray that God will channel that provocation into spiritual fruit from which many men and women will benefit, to the glory of his name.

A Final Provocation

Let's be clear with ourselves, and with each other, that no one makes up his or her mind about such a set of crucial issues simply on the basis of theological argument. We dare not flatter ourselves that we sit on some intellectual height, calmly weighing each item in the balance of our finely calibrated intellects and entirely sanctified souls. We are all helplessly and thoroughly invested in a particular set of assumptions about gender, whatever that set may be. We are all enmeshed in social structures that reward or punish us because of our sex and because of our views of gender. We simply cannot be disinterested as we decide about this huge, and hugely important, set of issues. So let us own up to those facts, and let us ask ourselves these questions:

What do I really *want* to believe about gender?

Why do I want to believe that?[35]

In particular, what do I think I have to gain or lose by coming to this or that conclusion?

What are the voices in my head telling me to decide on one or another alternative, and how do I feel about each one?

Then we can ask this question in response: What shall I do to compensate for my own predispositions, limitations, and desires in order to hear the voice of God as clearly, searchingly, and transformationally as possible?

We will make no progress on this question if we do not open our hearts, as well as our minds, to the Spirit of God, in the good company of fellow Christians, with the attitude of submission to whatever God will say to us. The cross stands over us here as it does everywhere.

We simply must follow the example of young Samuel: "Speak, for your servant is listening" (1 Sam. 3:10).

And of young Mary: "Here am I, the servant of the Lord; let it be with me according to your word" (Luke 1:38).

35. For two very different reflections on this question—one personal and impressionistic, the other social scientific—see Nicholas Wolterstorff, "Between the Times," *Reformed Journal* 40 (December 1990): 18–19; and Gallagher, *Evangelical Identity and Gendered Family Life.* Both of these observers go beyond the question of individual prejudices and interests to remark on the social dimension: For some Christian groups, gender questions have become "boundary" and "identity" markers linked to even more fundamental matters of religious authority, theological method, and resistance to worldliness. As such, gender questions become almost impossibly large to submit to serious reexamination—and so they aren't.

Appendix A

How *Not* to Decide about Gender

Many authors writing on the question of Christianity and gender have located their discussion within the broader context of hermeneutics—the discipline of interpreting the Bible and applying it to contemporary issues.[1] At the same time, it is actually quite remarkable how many do not. Instead, they immediately plunge into exegetical and historical issues as if there are no important methodological questions to sort out first. As Pamela Dickey Young reminds us, however, "One's

---

1. Some good examples are the following: Robert K. Johnston, "The Role of Women in the Church and Home: An Evangelical Testcase in Hermeneutics," in *Scripture, Tradition, and Interpretation*, ed. W. Ward Gasque and William Sanford LaSor, 234–59 (Grand Rapids: Eerdmans, 1978)—I register my debt to this remarkably fair-minded essay that affected my early thinking on this question; Ronald W. Pierce, Rebecca Merrill Groothuis, and Gordon D. Fee, eds., *Discovering Biblical Equality: Complementarity without Hierarchy* (Downers Grove, IL: InterVarsity, 2004); Willard M. Swartley, *Slavery, Sabbath, War, and Women: Case Issues in Biblical Interpretation* (Scottdale, PA: Herald, 1983); Mary Stewart Van Leeuwen, ed., *After Eden: Facing the Challenge of Gender Reconciliation* (Grand Rapids: Eerdmans, 1993); and William J. Webb, *Slaves, Women, and Homosexuals* (Downers Grove, IL: InterVarsity, 2001).

theological method in large part determines one's theological outcome."[2] If one generally assumes, for example, that Old Testament law is to apply to Christians today directly and without adaptation, then one will be led to certain conclusions about gender. If one assumes that the portraits of Jesus in the Gospels are the final interpretative norm in Scripture, then one will necessarily entertain only a certain range of interpretative options. If one assumes that contemporary natural and social science shed important light on the matter, then one will see questions of gender differently.

Rather than attempting to provide a general summary of hermeneutical wisdom, I want to offer some basic reflections on the common ways people deal *badly* with the question of gender in the hope that readers will seek a better way.

Many people, it seems, are impatient with discussion of methodology when the issue of gender arises. Indeed, they do not understand why it has to arise at all. They mistakenly believe that the question of whether Christianity is compatible with feminism has already been resolved—and resolved easily. Some believe it has been resolved in favor of compatibility, as in "Of course Christians can be feminists!" Others believe it has been resolved in favor of mutual exclusivity: "You're either a genuine Christian or a feminist. You can't be both."

The controversy, however, continues. My point here is that it cannot be settled, as some believe it can be, merely by recourse to one of three favorite interpretative shortcuts: biblicism, reference to the common wisdom of contemporary society, and personal intuition.

Biblicism: "The Bible Says So"

There is a long-standing form of Christian piety, commonly found especially among Protestants, whose adherents congratulate themselves for their fidelity to the Bible against all other

2. Pamela Dickey Young, *Feminist Theology/Christian Theology: In Search of Method* (Minneapolis: Fortress, 1990), 17.

voices. "No creed but the Bible," they say, or perhaps "*sola scriptura*," if they like to add the gloss of tradition. "The Bible says it; I believe it; that settles it" speaks directly for many. Yet such "Bible-believing" Christians are fooling themselves when they claim to interpret and practice simply what the Bible says. For one thing, they fail to realize they are defending their own interpretations, not the Bible itself. Indeed, so great is their confidence that they can simply read the Bible—a compilation of dozens of ancient books, composed originally in now-dead languages that no one can even confidently pronounce, from a variety of countries, authors, and contexts—that they are surprised and even offended when someone indicates that they merely possess their own *interpretation* of this complicated literature, not its full and final meaning.

Folk piety among such Christians often affirms that the Bible is so clear that a little child can read it. (Occasionally, one finds this idea dressed up as "the perspicuity of Scripture.") Like much of folklore generally, this is partly true and also importantly false. Yes, someone of very limited intellectual ability can hear or read the Bible and be blessed by its profound simplicities: God is love, you shall have no other gods before me, Jesus is Lord, and so on. But God gave his people teachers, as the Bible itself affirms, precisely because much of the Bible is *not* easily understood.

Champions of mere biblicism occasionally claim sophisticated company with champions such as Tertullian ("I believe because it is absurd") and Søren Kierkegaard. But these notables are among the few eminent Christians who can be invoked in such a cause, and even then they are misunderstood, for these Christian thinkers valued reason so much that they employed quite a lot of it in their theological writings. Like the apostle Paul himself, who is occasionally invoked in this regard (so 1 Cor. 1:18–31), these great Christian thinkers opposed intellectual vanity and dependence on wisdom other than God's. They had no quarrel with reason, philosophy, and other intellectual disciplines when rightly deployed in God's service.

Instead, we should value all God's intellectual gifts to us. John Wesley built on his Anglican heritage of emphasizing Scripture, reason, and tradition (as Richard Hooker had put it) by adding experience to the theological mix. These four resources opened various windows into reality, and all should be received and employed with thanksgiving and the confidence that God speaks through all of them to help us understand and obey him. To be sure, Scripture is the privileged member of this set: No Christian safely decides against what he or she understands Scripture to say, since God has specially blessed Scripture as his written revelation. Still, because we are human beings with limited intellectual capacities and, worse, are still subject to the influence of sin, we must be aware of the fact that our interpretations of *anything*, including Scripture, may be possibly mistaken and even self-serving. God thus gives us a variety of epistemological checks and balances in these four resources. It is not, then, especially pious to refuse to use what God has given us in tradition, reason, and experience in favor of an exclusive use of Scripture. To do so is both foolish and ungrateful.

Sophisticated forms of this ungrateful foolishness are apparent in the Christian gender debate. Time and again, defenders of patriarchy will campaign on the grounds that "the Bible says so," as if that should suffice. But if what we *think* the Bible says (that is, our interpretation) seems contrary to one or more of the other intellectual resources God has given us, should we not pause to consider whether we have made a mistake somewhere—perhaps in our interpretation of secular reason or spiritual experience but also perhaps in our interpretation of the Bible?

Particularly in the case of gender distinctions, we should pause to consider a general characteristic of God's Word and God's commandments in particular. God speaks not only what is "right" but also what is "good." Let's hear again the familiar words of Psalm 19:7–9:

> The law of the LORD is perfect,
>   reviving the soul;
> the decrees of the LORD are sure,
>   making wise the simple;
> the precepts of the LORD are right,
>   rejoicing the heart;

the commandment of the LORD is clear,
    enlightening the eyes;
the fear of the LORD is pure,
    enduring forever;
the ordinances of the LORD are true
    and righteous altogether.

The psalmist commends God's Word not as opaque "divine command"—to be obeyed whether or not it appears to be good—but as transparently commendable wisdom on grounds appreciable by all. God's law appeals to us as healthy, strong, informative, joyful, corrective, holy, and so on.

Normally, then, when God commands something, we can see why it makes sense for him to do so. His written Word normally does not contradict but rather illuminates and harmonizes with his self-expression in other media, whether experience, reason, or religious tradition. To be sure, sometimes God's Word comes to us as a rebuke of our mistakes and sins, but even then we are equipped by the Spirit to recognize it as God's Word and as true and good.

When it comes to the question of gender, therefore, we can properly ask ourselves, Why is this commandment of the Lord *good* as well as right? If our interpretation of God's Word seems to result in something *bad*, it may be that it is our own badness that is being confronted and needs reorientation. It may also be that we have interpreted God's good Word *badly*.

As a sort of diagnostic test, then, perhaps we can consider these "sentence stems" to see whether they illuminate one or another interpretation of gender as good or bad:

"It is better for church government to have only men and no women because . . ."

"It is better to listen only to male preachers and never to female preachers because . . ."

"It is better for all church meetings for men, not women, to lead in prayer, liturgy, music, and so on because . . ."

"It is important to make sure that a woman who does participate in public worship has a man 'over her' in some authoritative role because . . ."

Can these stems be completed patriarchally in any way that makes sense other than "because the Bible [as we interpret it] says so"? I do not believe they can.

God's Word may be calling us to change our minds, to revise our expectations, to reframe issues we have sinfully or at least confusedly misunderstood. But it also may be that as we use our God-given reason, drawing on the experiences God has given us, we will not defy God's Word but instead come to understand it better and thus purge ourselves of erroneous interpretations. In this regard, it seems that the burden of proof falls on complementarians to show how it is really better for subordination to continue to characterize the relationship of Christian men and women.

Cultural Conformity or Nonconformity: "Society Says So"

Society's values cannot be assumed to be fully right, for society has previously taught us lots of things that we now believe are wrong: that women are not entitled to legal or political recognition, that non-Caucasians are eligible for exploitation, that the poor are not entitled to assistance, and so on. Society has said prohibition is bad, then good, then bad again. Society has said that governmental sponsorship of religion is good, then sometimes good, then bad. And so on.

Nor, however, can society's values be assumed to be wrong, as many alienated conservative Christians seem to feel, since many of those values have emerged from a Christian cultural matrix. Furthermore, many other religions and philosophies share at least some values with the Bible, so there is often common ground on which to make common cause.

We therefore cannot simply generalize in the form of "Society currently says x, and therefore x is right." Nor can we say the opposite: "and therefore x is wrong." The world is a place of ideological contest in which forces of good and evil contend and in which the dividing line of good and evil is drawn right through our own hearts—both individually and corporately. There is no entirely bad society on record, and there is no entirely good one either. We must exercise discernment, taking each case on its own terms and seeking God's enlightenment as to what is his will in this instance.

Thus, when it comes to the matter of gender, we must not unreflectively assume that what society says about women and men is right. For one thing, society is not speaking with a single voice about gender. Women are executives, but they are also regularly portrayed as bimbos and worse in sectors of popular culture. Women are leaders, but when they want to be mothers also, society has yet to accommodate them well. Women and men are just the same and also profoundly and universally different. It is not actually clear just what contemporary society is saying about gender.

Furthermore, society says a number of other things in this sphere and related ones that most Christians believe are patently false: that homosexuality is natural and normal, that sexual intercourse can be merely recreational, that cohabiting is a good preparation for marriage, that amicable divorces are better for children than unhappy marriages, and so on.

Yet society has in many respects come to speak more Christianly about a variety of subjects over the last decades than it had in ostensibly more Christian days. Compare today with a hundred years ago and ask yourself whether Christian values are more or less evident in how we treat handicapped people, non-Caucasians, and the unemployed. Gospel values are still evident and even growing in some sectors of contemporary life—the worldwide spread of the language of universal human rights is a great trend forward—at the same time as other Christian values seem to be eroding.

We need to do our homework in any given case, without taking our cues automatically—whether positively or negatively—from what society happens to be doing or saying today.

Intuition: "The Spirit Says So"

Because church tradition, societal practice, and the heritage of biblical interpretation all seemed against them, many women seeking greater freedom in Christian service relied on their inner sense of God's leading. These women were not always radicals in the heat of evangelical revivals, or on the fringes of medieval monasticism, or in the netherworld of the cults (what we more politely refer to nowadays as "new religious movements"). These women show up as respectable nuns, missionaries, Bible teachers, evangelists, and authors throughout church history. When they were called on to account for their ministry, many of them responded, "The Lord led me to it."[3]

This reliance on spiritual discernment is dangerous—as many of these women recognized themselves. One's personal intuitions—even, or perhaps especially, those that we think are from God—must be tested against the alternative possibilities of self-deception, demonic deception, and just plain misunderstanding (e.g., excessive or misguided application of a genuinely true word of God). The history of mysticism is replete with cautions and safeguards offered by spiritual masters who were well aware of the perils of misinterpreted experience. Mainstream Christian teaching affirms that one's intuitive sense of God's voice should be matched with Scripture, tradition, and reason—and in the company of other Christians—so as to minimize the danger of misunderstanding or misdirection and to maximize the blessing of a genuine divine communication.

In the current debate, therefore, there is little excuse for relying on sheer intuition when the theological resources are so extensive and the company of like-minded Christians—whatever view one has—is available, especially in the age of the Internet, relatively cheap telephone services, and so on. I do not mean that it is always and everywhere easy for people to think these things through. There are families, churches, and communities in which the consensus is so strong that anyone holding a deviant view—or even just considering an alternative—is under strong

3. For women in church history, see Lynda L. Coon, Katherine J. Haldane, and Elisabeth W. Sommer, eds., *That Gentle Strength: Historical Perspectives on Women in Christianity* (Charlottesville: University Press of Virginia, 1990); and Ruth A. Tucker and Walter Liefeld, *Daughters of the Church: Women and Ministry from New Testament Times to the Present* (Grand Rapids: Zondervan, 1987). For broader context still, see Denise Lardner Carmody, *Women and World Religions*, 2nd ed. (Englewood Cliffs, NJ: Prentice-Hall, 1989).

pressure, whether in a liberal situation in Manhattan or a conservative situation in Alabama. Still, however, most people can access resources to help them sort things through beyond what happens to "feel right" to them. And, again, because we finite and fallen human beings are so easily misled, we must not settle for facilely gained answers to important and vexed questions when God puts other resources within our reach.

Yet I am sympathetic to those women who, through the ages, have followed an inner voice into authentic Christian service, for what else could God's Spirit do to lead them to it, if not a direct intuition, in such extreme situations? Realistically, there was not much to work with, given the overwhelming and reinforcing consensus in scriptural interpretation, church teaching and practice, and societal patterns regarding patriarchy. So we do not have to condemn our sisters in the past for substandard theological methods. We can, instead, commend good theological method to our sisters (and brothers) today who want to make the best use of all God's gifts in order to come to the best conclusions possible.

Appendix B

A Woman's Place Is in ... Theology?

Most of the theological attention that Christians have paid to women has been focused on the nexus of issues at the heart of this book: gender in family, church, and society. But two other zones have been hotly contested as well.[1]

The first is the question of Bible translations: To what extent, if at all, should contemporary Bible translations reflect inclusive language for human beings? The second is the question of gendered language for God in liturgy, hymns, and so on: Should God be referred to always in masculine images (father, husband) and male pronouns? Both of these issues deserve another look—as does a third, which apparently is not a controversial issue among many traditional Christians (Catholic, Orthodox, and Protestant) but should be, namely, the pursuit of feminist theology.

---

1. Some material in what follows appeared originally in the following essays: "The Battle for the Inclusive Bible," *Christianity Today* 43 (November 15, 1999): 83–84; "Finding a Home for Eve," *Christianity Today* 43 (March 1, 1999): 60–61; and "God as Lord and Lover: Masculine Language Revisited," *Christian Century* 109 (November 11, 1992): 1020–21.

When it comes to Bible translation, as in the discussion of so many other intellectual and cultural questions, many conservative Christians live in a strange world. It is a sort of dark Alice-in-Wonderland landscape in which peaceful places can metamorphose hazardously at a moment's notice. At times, the landscape is fairly flat and stable. Lots of different people and communities and ideas and concerns exist together, with good-natured exchanges all 'round, including even the occasional sincere and civil disagreement. It is a sort of Serengeti waterhole of inclusivity. But sometimes the ground shifts abruptly, and traditional believers see themselves perched on top of a steep mountain of truth. From here, any step is a step down. Worse, any step risks a calamitous slide all the way down a slippery slope to wreckage at the other extreme. Such an earthquake has erupted in the green pastures of Bible translations.

In recent decades, Christians have produced a wide range of versions of the Scriptures they love. Yes, some of us have grumbled: "This one is too wooden"; "That one is too idiosyncratic." A colorful minority have entertained or bemused the rest of us with their defense of the King James Version (KJV) as if it were divinely inspired—ironically, in an argument not unlike conservative Roman Catholic defenses of Jerome's fourth-century Latin translation of Scripture, the Vulgate, which now enjoys the status of "inspired text" in Catholic tradition. But most Christians tolerate and many even rejoice in the diversity of translations.

At times, resistance to a translation has been more intense. Most significant and widespread among Protestants was the criticism of the Revised Standard Version (RSV), issued in the 1950s. Many Christians thought this translation manifested an ominous theological agenda—a liberal agenda that challenged the proper interpretation of such key doctrines as the virgin birth (so Isaiah 7:14 and "a young woman" instead of "a virgin") and the atonement (so 1 John 2:2 and 4:10 and the milder "expiation" for the King James Version's "propitiation"). Other Christians, however, were not convinced that the RSV was unfaithful to the Greek and Hebrew texts and therefore used it as a helpful alternative to the archaic—and therefore often *more* misleading—expression of the KJV.

In the last decade or so, North American Protestantism has been wracked with controversy over a different issue. Now the question is so-called inclusive language translations, those versions that have changed some or all of the Bible's generic masculine language to language that explicitly includes, or at least does not implicitly exclude, women. No more "mankind" or "man" or "he who will . . ." when all persons, not just males, are meant.

Interestingly, when the New Revised Standard Version (NRSV) was released in 1989, many Christians, including some evangelicals, were happy to use it as the first translation to apply such principles in a sweeping way. Most conservative Christians, however, simply ignored it. The earlier battle over the RSV perhaps had sorted things out: You either liked and used the RSV, or you did not, and the same would go for the NRSV.

The ground did not heave up until evangelicalism's most widely used modern translation, the New International Version, emerged as a significantly altered edition in 1995. Periodicals such as *World* magazine, Bible scholars such as complementarian Wayne Grudem, and popular leaders such as Focus on the Family's James Dobson sounded an alarm against what they saw to be a serious threat to—well, to what? Why had the rather peaceful plain of Bible translations—to each his own; there's room enough for all—tilted into a sheer cliff down which one would tumble if one surrendered one's position at the peak?

Several realities need recognition, realities that some of the zealots have failed to see clearly.[2] First, all translations have infelicities and even outright errors. Despite our best intentions, even in committees (and sometimes especially in committees), we human beings make mistakes. No translation is perfect.

2. Among helpful guides to this debate are two books by evangelical scholars who cannot be faulted for a feminist bias, since they are self-declared complementarians: Mark Strauss, *Distorting Scripture? The Challenge of Bible Translation and Gender Accuracy* (Downers Grove, IL: InterVarsity, 1998); and Donald Carson, *The Inclusive Language Debate: A Plea for Realism* (Grand Rapids: Baker Academic, 1998).

Second, translation is always approximate because no two languages can be converted exactly into each other. "The exact word" isn't ever quite *le mot juste.*

Third, and perhaps most important, translation of gender language is especially difficult nowadays because English usage is itself changing, and not changing everywhere at the same time in the same way. Some of us use "mankind" and others "humankind." Some of us use "he" generically; others scrupulously say "he or she"; and still others switch back and forth between "he" and "she." The translator, therefore, has unavoidable trouble trying to connect the fixed languages of biblical Hebrew and Greek with the moving target of contemporary English—one might even say, of contemporary English*es*.

Fourth, and perhaps most radically, some of us are making way too big a deal about relatively small changes. Yes, something is lost when a translation moves away from the image of the solitary godly person in Psalm 1 ("Blessed is the man who . . .") to the collective ("Blessed are those . . ."). But how much, really? Enough to warrant blasting a new version with a shotgun and mailing it back to the publisher? Enough to sanction threats to a Bible society if it does not cease producing the offending version? Enough to justify the dismissal of a seminary professor involved in the translation project a year before his retirement? Enough to keep a new translation out of the hands of people who would welcome it both for their own reading and for sharing the gospel with friends who may be sensitive to gender questions? (All of these have happened during the course of this controversy.)

Conservative New Testament scholar Donald Carson describes the disproportionate reaction of some critics as "Bible rage." One may well ask, then, since psychological and sociological categories beg to be employed here, What agenda could possibly be pressing people to such instant and insistent opposition?

Some critics openly articulate their fear that such inclusive translations represent the not-so-thin edge of a feminist wedge that will lead next to feminine language for God (not just for human beings) and from thence to outright goddess worship.

To be sure, there have been some moderating noises from this anxious camp. They allow that some changes can legitimately be made in translation where the original languages clearly mean—in their literal words, not just their phrases—to include both men and women. But they allow relatively few. Making too many, it seems, might set off an avalanche of gender chaos.

Yet the record shows that not one mainstream translation has crossed the line from inclusive language for human beings to feminine language for God. Even the NRSV preface explicitly acknowledges that the one sort of change does not entail the other. Furthermore, since the Bible's original languages themselves contain obviously feminine language about God, an extreme position on this matter ("let's stay in this ditch so we don't slide over into the other one") is indefensible, as we will discuss further in a moment.

A previous generation of evangelicals worried over the RSV because they felt that great matters of the gospel were at stake. However right or wrong they were about this perception, that controversy seems much more important than the anti-inclusive language crusade today. Today, it is simply not the case that we are presented with translations that portray God as a goddess. We are not presented with translations that try to "improve" on the Bible by conforming it to this or that ideology. The more-or-less level plain of legitimate translation alternatives has not been turned into an all-or-nothing cliff face of "Christian" at the top versus "anti-Christian" at the bottom. We instead have been gifted with a range of translations by earnest Christian scholars who have aimed at the edification of the church and the evangelization of the world.

Frankly, when it seems evident that Jesus himself used an Aramaic paraphrase of the Old Testament; when conservative Christians of all stripes enthusiastically support missionary Bible translators all over the world whose versions—because rendered by a few people with relatively few linguistic tools at hand—are always much less accurate than the English translations we are privileged to enjoy; and when hundreds of thousands of conservative evangelicals are buying and using such informal and free-wheeling paraphrases as the New Living Bible and *The Message*, it is difficult to believe that all this sound and fury truly centers on the question of the crystalline integrity of Bible translation.

So if it is not really about translation, then North American Christians confront a hard question. Has the fervor in this latest battle for the Bible instead been aroused by the clash of social and political agendas? Have Bible-loving Christians succumbed to the temptation to co-opt the dignity of God's Word for something much less ultimate, much less certain, and much less glorious—namely, the explicitly antifeminist patriarchalism so important to these critics?

The second issue gives many feminist Christians pause as well: the question of inclusive language for God.

Those of us who, like me, persist in reading the Bible as a revelation from God as well as a human account of this revelation encounter many difficulties, if not offenses, in this apparent hodgepodge of ancient literature. One vexing question that has troubled many such readers—as well as less traditional ones—is the self-description of God in masculine terms.

Yes, God is spirit, and most serious theologians of every age have dismissed the idea that God has genitalia or other indications of human maleness. Yes, there are wonderful passages in the Bible that speak of God's "femaleness" (specifically as a mother bird [e.g., Deut. 32:11; Matt. 23:37]). But recent scholarship has largely underscored that the dominant biblical portrait of God is drawn with male imagery. Therefore, what is a culturally and personally sensitive theologian to do with what seems, frankly, to be an embarrassment? Why did God reveal Godself almost all the time as "himself" and not "herself" or "itself" or "him/herself"?

Even those of us who maintain a traditional understanding of inspiration believe that in the Bible God accommodates his ideas and ways to our little human minds and hearts. That is, the Bible does not tell us about the Most High God in ways that would be beyond our understanding. The Bible, as God's Word *to us*, speaks of God as God is to, and toward, us.

If we try to "think God's thoughts after him," why might God select this sort of language almost all the time for self-description? I would suggest that from the beginning of revelation

God has tried to get two main points about Godself across to human beings. The first is that God is transcendent, almighty, self-existent; the creator and sustainer of all things, author of history, upholder of righteousness, judge of the earth, consummator of the ages. How would God best communicate this point to people in the cultures of the Old and New Testaments? By using the image of lord, ruler, monarch, judge, master—images of positions that were, in those cultures, generally held by males.

The second and complementary point God has tried to get across to us is that God cares deeply about human beings as well as the rest of creation. God made us, looks after us, disciplines us, and draws us into renewed fellowship with Godself. In particular, God chooses and cherishes a people, establishes with them a covenant of care, and seeks to forge with them an eternal bond of faithful, mutual devotion. How to get this across to people in the cultures of the Old and New Testaments? By using the image of lover—of parent, yes, but even more of suitor and spouse.

To combine the ideas of lord and lover surely would require masculine imagery for the most part. In cultures in which men take the initiative in courtship, having to woo and win the bride (normally with the consent of her parents), the image of a male suitor works most naturally. In cultures in which husbands and fathers rule their households and provide materially for them and defend them, the masculine image of lord works most naturally.

If Yahweh instead had a consort like Asherah, he would have a divine counterpart to love. Thus, the striking, even scandalous, biblical image of God seeking a bride in the people of Israel would make no sense. If God were to reveal Godself as asexual or as simultaneously and equally masculine and feminine, there again would be no grounds on which to relate God to humanity in the image of a spouse.

Does this imagery of suitor and husband mean that God in some fundamental sense *needs* his people the way human husbands need their wives? Does God's joy and fulfillment really depend on the faithful devotion of his spouse? Many Christians harrumph at this point and say, "No! God needs nothing, and he certainly doesn't need us."

The Bible, however, seems to say that he *does* need us in an important way. "As the bridegroom rejoices over the bride, so shall your God rejoice over you" (Isa. 62:5). "Husbands, love your wives, just as Christ loved the church and gave himself up for her. . . . For no one ever hates his own body, but he nourishes and tenderly cares for it, just as Christ does for the church" (Eph. 5:25, 29). Metaphysical affirmations (such as God's "aseity") notwithstanding, God has bound himself to his people with love, and it is the love of (one speaks carefully here) companions—even virtual equals, virtual peers. This is the relationship of husbands and wives.

"Virtual" is an important qualifier, since God clearly is the greater partner in the relationship. It would be inappropriate, however, exclusively to use the language of parent and child. Though this terminology does depict some aspects of the divine/human relationship, it does not convey God's complete investment in and hope for a lifelong relationship of mutuality. Surely only marriage imagery can work this way, and in the context of biblical times, which included both mutuality and hierarchy in male/female relations, only lord and lover imagery would work. So the question is this: If you had been God then, what would you have done to convey these ideas?

One may still fairly raise a host of counterquestions, including whether this imagery has served and still serves to perpetuate unjust relations between men and women, whom we understand today to be equals, not virtual equals. Those of us who believe that God has *not* permanently ordained patriarchy in church, society, or home have some work to do to explain our position to both our liberal friends and our conservative ones—which I have done in this book. I have tried to show how one can responsibly affirm both egalitarianism *and* the Bible's images for the divine/human relationship in patriarchal terms.

Perhaps this brief reflection raises a cautionary note regarding the semantics of theology, liturgy, and so on. Changing an element here often means an implicit change there, one we may not in fact want to make. Yes, we need to affirm—and perhaps affirm more often than we do—that God is not male. We need to recognize that the biblical accounts need reinterpretation from points of view other than that of the traditional privileged male. But let us also appreciate the multidimensional images of the Bible that contain important truths in helpful, balanced combination, such as the language of lord and lover. If we are going to go beyond biblical images as we attempt to theologize in contemporary, nonpatriarchal terms, we must make sure that our alternatives maintain the best elements of the biblical system and do so in their appropriate relations. This is always the challenge in improving on the tradition of our elders (let alone on the revelation of God). It often emerges that they knew more than we may think, and we would do well not to dispense quickly with their wisdom.

With this cautionary note still in the air, let us confront the fact that among conservative Christians today there is all too little imaginative and scholarly exploration of new ways, *feminist* ways, of reading the Bible and constructing theology.[3]

Feminism, like all advocacy, is centrally about absence and presence. It is about recognizing that people who have been ignored and marginalized are right here, and there, and everywhere. If women are *not* everywhere, then feminism asks, Where are they?[4]

3. Roman Catholics follow the direction laid out by John Paul II to forge a feminism that is both traditional—patriarchal in some respects, especially in regard to clergy—and yet also affirming of women as fully human beings. It remains to be seen how feminist this is and how much it is just the Catholic version of Protestant complementarianism. Still, it is a more robust and extensive philosophical and theological program than is evident among Protestants. See Michele M. Schumacher, ed., *Women in Christ: Toward a New Feminism* (Grand Rapids: Eerdmans, 2004). Cf. Hans Küng, *Women in Christianity*, trans. John Bowden (New York: Continuum, 2001).

4. On the following, especially regarding feminist biblical studies, see Cullen Murphy, *The Word according to Eve: Women and the Bible in Ancient Times and Our Own* (New York: Houghton Mifflin, 1998). Murphy's book, it must be acknowledged, ranges no further to the right than the scholarship of Fuller Theological Seminary, which is commonly seen to represent the leftward edge of North American evangelicalism.

Roman Catholic theologian David Tracy has called feminist scholarship "the next intellectual revolution." Yet this revolution has hardly touched conservative Protestantism in the fields of biblical and theological studies. This phenomenon is odd, considering the burgeoning field of historical studies of American evangelical women—a major category of the more general rise of American evangelical history writing since 1980, led in particular by the efforts of the Wheaton College–based Institute for the Study of American Evangelicals. There is now a large supply of theses, dissertations, articles, and books on women in American evangelicalism, as there is on women in North American religion as a whole. But in biblical and theological scholarship, women seem absent, both as subjects and as scholars.

On the question of patriarchy versus egalitarianism in family and church, it is easy to point to Alvera Mickelsen, Gretchen Gaebelein Hull, Catherine Clark Kroeger, and other well-published biblical scholars. Social scientists such as psychologist Mary Stewart Van Leeuwen and sociologist Elaine Storkey have contributed much to this discourse as well. But when it comes to looking at broader questions of biblical interpretation and to the composition of fresh theological schemes, one still asks, Where are the women? And where are distinctive feminist concerns among the men?

It is not as if there is something inimical to conservative Christianity in a feminist approach to the Bible. One brief example can point the way. Let us take a critical, but also appreciative, look at one of the best-known books of feminist exegesis, namely, *Texts of Terror: Literary-Feminist Readings of Biblical Narratives* by the estimable Phyllis Trible, a former president of the Society of Biblical Literature.[5]

Old Testament scholar Walter Brueggemann—a favorite exegete among many evangelical and Catholic scholars and preachers—endorses this book in the foreword, a book that originated as the Beecher Lectures on preaching at Yale. Brueggemann extols it for getting "the interpreter-expositor out of the way so that the unhindered text and the listening community can

5. Philadelphia: Fortress, 1984.

face each other." Brueggemann continues, "The method utilized here makes very little, if any, imposition on the text. . . . There is no special pleading, no stacking of the cards, no shrillness, no insistence."[6]

Well, let's see. Facing the first page of the first chapter, the reader encounters an extraordinary illustration: a sketch of a tombstone, with Hagar's name inscribed above an epitaph, "Egyptian slave woman." Below this is the text, "She was wounded for our transgressions; she was bruised for our iniquities." Before Trible has even begun her exposition of the Hagar story, therefore, it may appear that the deck has indeed been stacked by something other than "the unhindered text"—namely, a controversial juxtaposition of Hagar's story and the messianic prophecy of Isaiah 53.

The book ends as it begins, as Trible composes a lament for Jephthah's daughter by rewriting on her behalf the lament of David over Saul and Jonathan (2 Sam. 1:19–27). Such imaginative composition may well be a worthy poetic response to the story, but when the interpreter/expositor decides that the best way to conclude her Bible study is with a nonbiblical text intended to compensate for the Bible's offensive silence regarding Jephthah's daughter, we must agree that we do not have merely the text and the listening community facing each other anymore.

In between, among her helpful insights, Trible often seems to be looking for trouble. For instance, as she concludes her study of the unnamed concubine who is raped, murdered, and dismembered at the end of the book of Judges, Trible pronounces, "Truly, to speak for this woman is to interpret against the narrator, plot, other characters, and the biblical tradition because they have shown her neither compassion nor attention."[7] She goes on to praise the subsequent stories of Hannah and Ruth as showing "both the Almighty and the male establishment a more excellent way."[8] This suggestion that parts of the Bible

6. Ibid., ix–x.
7. Ibid., 86.
8. Ibid., 85.

should be read against each other and are instructive even for God is nonsense for traditional Christians who understand God to be the Author of the Bible behind and within all the various human writers of its component parts. This sort of interpretative stance cannot assist such Christians in an appropriate feminist interest in Scripture.

Yet what would feminist exposition look like that saw God as the ultimate Author of the Bible? Trible thinks the Bible's refusal to name this woman dishonors her. But perhaps the anonymity is a device to underscore her insignificance in the eyes of the violent men in the narrative rather than to imply that she is insignificant in the eyes of God, for how can a Christian believe such a woman could be insignificant to the Father of our Lord Jesus Christ? Trible suggests that such horrors are described in Judges in order to buttress the case for kingship under Saul or David, who each went on to commit atrocities of his own. But, again, a narrator who is inspired by the Narrator would be heard instead as confirming Trible's own point: Sin is vile and vigorous, and no mere political scheme will compensate for resistance to God's law. Such a lesson does not show even these putatively "terrible" parts of the Bible to be misogynistic but quite the opposite.

Phyllis Trible, it should be remembered, is among the more conservative feminist scholars widely admired in the broader academic study of the Bible.[9] What comes across again and again in such scholarship is an absence: the absence of God as the Author of Scripture. Without the unifying force of a single authorial voice holding it together, the Bible can indeed fall apart into a welter of apparent contradictions and scandals.

To affirm the presence of God's voice in Scripture, however, is automatic for evangelicals, conservative Catholics, and other traditional Christians. In this brief interaction with Trible from an evangelical point of view, therefore, I trust it is evident that traditional Christians can both benefit from the lead taken by

9. For a taste of things to Trible's left that covers many of the same stories, see Danna Nolan Fewell and David M. Gunn, *Gender, Power, and Promise: The Subject of the Bible's First Story* (Nashville: Abingdon, 1993). I thank Phil Long for this reference.

scholars such as she and also contribute exegetical insights of their own based on their different methodological and theological presuppositions. Trible's is not the only feminist approach to the Bible. Orthodox Christians can and should develop their own.

At the same time, most evangelicals and Roman Catholics have not been so quick to affirm the presence of women. Therefore, we might pause to consider another conspicuous absence in the discussion of women and the Bible, namely, the lack of impact more than a generation of feminist studies has made on most orthodox Christian theology.

In our churches, of course, and in popular writing and speaking, the contemporary feminist movement has garnered a great deal of attention. Congregations and denominations have split over the ordination of women, and entire organizations have been founded to campaign for one or another viewpoint on gender. But beyond the political question of which sex plays which roles in the church or in the family, feminist thinking seems yet unable to find a home in orthodox theology.

Even among those orthodox theologians who seem most open to contemporary currents in theology—whether process thought, liberationism, postliberalism, and so on—and who call for renewal or "revisioning" of orthodox theology, feminist analysis is scarcely evident. But if good fruit can be harvested from these other nonorthodox theological discourses, why not from feminist studies?[10]

Consider the female figure of Wisdom in the Bible. This intriguing subject should not be left to those seeking a goddess to complement the ("male") God of the Bible. What about the female imagery used in the Bible to depict divine care for

10. Cherith Fee Nordling, among the few North American evangelical scholars to become familiar with a wide range of feminist theologies, notes that evangelical avoidance of feminist work is mirrored by typical feminist avoidance of nonfeminist work: "Much feminist theology is poor—not because it is feminist, but because it fails to uphold a high standard of scholarship. Feminist theology is most often dualistically constructed from the perspective of 'us' and 'them'—the oppressed and the oppressors—and their methodology reflects this dualism. Women who write theological treatises without consulting works by non-feminists (or men, period) . . . limit full-fledged engagement within the disciplines of

God's people? We have seen above that this is an important, if relatively minor, motif in Scripture: So how do "Bible-believing" Christians acknowledge it properly? How would a feminist point of view help us consider any one of a number of theological issues, whether the atonement, the work of the Holy Spirit, the scope of salvation, or the nature of the world to come? Surely, feminist insights can help improve such key Christian conversations as those regarding congregational life (beyond leadership issues), liturgy, apologetics, and our use of money. We do not know what feminist thought could give us because few orthodox Christians are investigating it, and those who are typically do so without the support of their faith communities, who are generally suspicious of anything of this sort.

Orthodox Christians affirm that God is not sexual and is neither male nor female or, perhaps better, that God is imaged in *both* male and female human beings together. We affirm that doctrine readily and then go ahead and depict God as male—not *mostly* as male, the way the Bible does, but *always* as male. As a rule, it seems, orthodox Christians *never* depict God as female, even metaphorically, and rarely even as transcending the categories of male and female. But the Bible does.

Many of us do something similar in our treatment of one another. We are happy to affirm for the record that men are not inherently superior to women, that male and female together are created in the *imago Dei*. But then we *act* as if males really are superior—superior as topics for Bible study, superior to lead in

---

theology and Biblical studies. . . . By creating a sub-discipline through reading and responding only to other feminists, these women fall into the same traps of the tradition they criticize. When theology is done only in the company of like minds and like interests, it perpetuates a narrow view maintained from a moral high ground. The humility, kindness, and openness necessary to learn from differently positioned texts and conversation partners seems absent from much feminist dialogue. And yet, if this is so, how will those who might benefit most from exposure to their perspective ever really gain access to [it]?" (correspondence with the author, March 2005). An unwitting witness to Fee Nordling's testimony is provided by a survey of feminist theology that is almost completely unaware of any evangelical scholarship on the question at all: Natalie K. Watson, *Feminist Theology* (Grand Rapids: Eerdmans, 2003).

church and home, even superior to represent all human beings (as in the so-called generic language of "mankind"). Where are the women? More basically, where is the female, the feminine, the not-male in the Bible, in our churches and families, and in God? We must resist contemporary extremes such as lesbian marriages and goddess worship. We must resist the loss of rich biblical truth encoded in masculine language for God in the Bible and in traditional theology. But our fear of those losses must not keep us in a masculinist extreme. We must encourage more women to undertake careers in theological scholarship. We must hear women's voices in our churches. We men must ask feminist questions along with our more standard lines of intellectual interrogation. We must pray for God to forgive us our sexist sins, heal our blindness, motivate our hearts, and open our minds. If the women are absent in biblical and theological studies, we all are missing out on half of the Story.[11]

---

11. Indeed, we are missing much more than half, given the historic statistical overrepresentation of women in the church, as in religion generally. Symbolically, politically, and in most other ways, of course, women have been *under*represented. See Rodney Stark, with Alan S. Miller, "Faith and Gender," in *Exploring the Religious Life* (Baltimore: Johns Hopkins University Press, 2004), 60–83.

Subject Index

abuse, 12, 27n13, 59, 100
accommodation, principle of, 60, 84,
  89n25, 92–99, 120
  and church, 52n13, 57, 89n25, 92,
  96–97
  and culture, 10–11n1, 87
  and God, 39–41, 64–65
  See also patriarchy:
  accommodation of
activism, principle of, 97–98, 101
amelioration of inequality, 10–11n1,
  45, 57, 61, 65, 84, 96
Applebaum, Patricia, 56n18
Aquinas, Thomas, 25n9

Basinger, David, 81n10
Beauvoir, Simone de, 85
Beaver, R. Pierce, 83n15
Belleville, Linda L., 52n13
Benne, Robert, 87
Bergman, Susan, 83n13
Bible 28–38, 52n13, 72, 92, 96, 102
  and control texts, 28
  and images of God, 78–79, 120–23
  and inclusive language, 118–23
  interpretation of, 10–11n1, 12–13,
  24, 31–34, 68, 106–9, 111–12, 124–
  26

and justice, 19–20n5
and pattern of doubleness, 63–70,
  87
and sexism, 12–13
translations of, 115–20
See also feminism: and Scripture;
  gender: and Bible; hermeneutics;
  patriarchy: and Scripture
biblicism, 106–10
Bonhoeffer, Dietrich, 96
Bruce, F. F., 52n13
Brueggemann, Walter, 124
Buckley, Jack, 35n1

Calvin, John, 47
Carmichael, Amy, 45n11
Carmody, Denise Lardner, 112n3
Carson, Donald, 117–8
Carter, Stephen, 27n13, 86
church
  and feminism, 16, 38, 56, 80–81, 96
  and gender roles, 11, 15–16, 20–29,
  32–37, 49–59, 67–71, 83–84, 109–
  12, 127–29
  and patriarchy, 13n4, 37, 52n13,
  55–56, 65, 78–80, 97–100, 122–24
  and scriptural interpretation, 24,
  27–28

and slavery, 58
and values, 45
See also accommodation, principle
  of: and church; egalitarians: and
  the church; gender debate: and
  church history; women: and
  church
Clement of Alexandria, 25n9
complementarians, 17–18, 19, 36–37,
  41, 50, 67n28, 70–72, 90–91, 110
  and church history, 82–84
  and feminism, 24–29, 55
  and marriage, 60–61, 88
  and Paul, 51, 68
  and theology, 76–80
Coon, Linda L., 112n3
Cox, Kendall, 11, 12n2
creation mandate, 35, 67n28

Davids, Peter, 70n30
Dayton, Donald W., 56n18
DeBerg, Betty A., 84–85n16
Dobson, James, 117
Doriani, Dan, 71–72n33

Edwards, Jonathan, 26n12
egalitarians, 12, 17–19, 20n5, 41–42
  and the church, 51–56, 99
  and the home, 57–63
  and marriage, 88
  and modern society, 55–56, 72, 84
  and patriarchy, 27, 49, 69–71, 92,
    124
  and Scripture, 29–30, 35–38, 50–51,
    63, 67–69, 122
  and theology, 76–81
  See also equality; feminism;
    feminist
Elliot, Elisabeth, 84
epistemological warrants, 23, 76n1
equality, 10–11n1, 19–20n5, 35–38,
  56n18, 67n28, 68, 70, 72, 84, 92
eschatology, 41–42, 93–94, 101–2
evangelicals, 12, 26n12, 34, 38n3, 82,
  117, 119, 126–27

Fee, Gordon, 52n13, 54–55n15,
  105n1
feminism, 15, 18n3, 48, 56n18, 57,
  77n3, 89, 99, 106
  and children, 90–92
  Christian feminism, 10, 12, 15–16,
    78, 84–86, 94, 96
  and language, 120–23
  and Scripture, 16–17, 38n3, 40–41,
    63, 118, 123–29
  secular feminism, 84–86
  and social pathologies, 16, 81–84,
    111–12
  and theology, 115, 123–29
  See also church: and feminism
feminist, 17, 34–35. See also egalitarians; feminism
Fewell, Danna Nolan, 126n9
Finney, Charles, 83
Flanagan, Caitlin, 90n27
Friedan, Betty, 85

Gallagher, Sally K., 84–85n16,
  103n35
Gasque, Laurel, 52n13
Gasque, W. Ward, 52n13, 105n1
Gay, Craig M., 81n8
gender, 17n2
  and Bible, 29, 66–70, 87, 102, 109
  differences of, 17, 18n3, 25, 29, 35,
    57, 61–62, 71–72, 80–81, 88, 108,
    111
  and family, 11, 16, 34, 60, 90–92,
    94, 115, 124
  and Jesus, 36–38, 40–41, 51, 64, 69,
    79–80, 98
  and language, 78n5, 115, 118
  new understanding of (paradigm
    of), 35–50
  and Paul, 51–54
  and roles, 9, 11, 34–35, 62, 66–67,
    70, 92, 110, 127
  and society, 22, 111
  and spiritual gifts, 36, 50, 53, 56
  and views, 102–3

See also church: and gender roles;
    women
gender debate, 9–11, 13n4, 20–23, 34,
    49, 102, 108, 112–13
    and church history, 81–86, 102
    and feminist arguments, 24–28
    and methodological issues, 105–6
    and theology, 76–81
gospel, 28, 45, 49, 57, 86, 111, 118–19
    furtherance of, 47, 55, 88n22, 97
    priorities, 38–42, 53, 56n17, 63, 94–
    97
Gray, John, 25n10
Grenz, Stanley, 81n9, 89n24
Groothuis, Rebecca Merrill, 52n13,
    105n1
Grudem, Wayne, 117
Gunn, David M., 126n9

Habermas, Jürgen, 18n3
Haldane, Katherine J., 112n3
Hampl, Patricia, 83n13
Hancock, Maxine, 54–55n15
Hardesty, Nancy A., 56n18
Hassey, Janette, 83n14
hermeneutics, 65, 68, 79, 105–6
    and hermeneutical circle, 30
    "redemptive-movement
        hermeneutic," 10–11n1
Hildegard of Bingen, 83
Holifield, E. Brooks, 59n22
Holy Spirit, 24, 27–28, 32, 36, 39, 45,
    49, 51, 57, 61–62, 69, 84, 99, 109,
    113, 128
homosexuality, 86–90, 111
Hooker, Richard, 108
hope, principle of, 98
Hull, Gretchen Gaebelein, 67n28,
    94, 124
Hutchinson, Anne, 83

induction, method of, 31–32
Ingersoll, Julie, 84–85n16
intuition, use of, 28, 71n31, 106,
    111–13
Irigaray, Luce, 18n3

Jenkins, Philip, 95–96n32
Jerome, 25n9
Jewett, Paul, 38n3
John Paul II, 123n3
Johnston, Robert K., 105n1
Julian of Norwich, 41, 83

Kassian, Mary A., 84–85n16
Kempe, Margery, 83
Kierkegaard, Søren, 107
kingdom of God, 28, 36, 40–42, 45,
    49, 54, 72, 84, 98–101
Kjesbo, Denise Muir, 81n9
Kroeger, Catherine Clark, 52n13,
    100n34, 124
Kroeger, Richard Clark, 52n13
Kuhn, Thomas, 22
Küng, Hans, 123n3

LaSor, William Sanford, 105n1
Latourette, Kenneth Scott, 45n11
Lewis, C. S., 78n5, 79n7
liberty, 46–49, 51, 91, 100
Liefeld, Walter, 112n3
Long, Phil, 126n9
Lotz, Anne Graham, 84

marriage, 35, 37, 57, 59–61, 63, 66,
    79, 87–88, 95, 97–100, 111, 122
Marsden, George M., 26n12
Marshall, I. Howard, 62n24
Martin, David, 39
Martin, Walter R., 82n12
Maxwell, L. E., 55n16
McDermott, Gerald, 87
men
    and authority, 16, 60
    and "headship," 27n13
    and leadership, 26n12, 27, 71–72
    and power, 96
    and superiority, 67
Mickelsen, Alvera, 67n28, 124
Miller, Alan S., 129n11
Mouw, Richard J., 86n19
Murphy, Cullen, 123n4

Nason-Clark, Nancy, 100n34
Neill, Stephen, 45n11
Niebuhr, H. Richard, 56n17
Noll, Mark A., 59n22
Nordling, Cherith Fee, 127–28n10

Orthodox (Eastern), 11, 115, 127–28

Packer, J. I., 79n7
parent-child relations, 57, 59, 122
patriarchalists. *See* complementarians
patriarchy, 15–16, 27, 48–49, 52n13,
    57, 67n28, 108, 113, 122, 124
  accommodation of, 10–11n1, 39–
    40, 52n13, 54–57, 60–65, 84, 87,
    92–96 (*see also* accommodation,
    principle of)
  eradication of, 10–11n1, 13n4, 42,
    57, 78–79
  and marriage, 59
  and Paul, 51–54, 66–69
  and Peter, 69–70
  response to, 97–101
  as result of the fall, 57, 93
  and Scripture, 37, 72, 78–81, 108–
    10
  See also church: and patriarchy;
    egalitarians: and patriarchy
Paul, apostle, 29–30, 36–38, 42–43,
    46–54, 59–61, 66–69, 78, 102, 107
Pelikan, Jaroslav, 24
perichoresis, 77n2
Peter, apostle, 43, 62–63
Pierce, Ronald W., 52n13, 105n1
piety, 9, 106–7
Plantinga, Cornelius, 93
Plymouth Brethren, 20–21
polygamy, 88, 94–95
pragmatism, 38–42
Provan, Iain, 64
providence, of God, 39–40, 52n13,
    72, 85

realism, principle of, 95, 97–99
redemption, 10–11n1, 36, 41, 47, 76,
    92–93

Schmidt, Thomas, 89n24
Schneiders, Sandra, 17n1
Scholer, David, 62n25
Schumacher, Michael M., 123n3
shalom, 36, 39, 41, 45, 86, 93, 96–98
sin, 41, 49, 57, 92–96, 108–9, 112,
    126
slavery, 10–11n1, 29, 41, 44n10,
    57–60, 62n24, 72, 87, 89, 95
Slessor, Mary, 45n11
Smith, Christian, 61n23
social conservatism, 42, 57–58
social science, 9, 92, 106
Stark, Rodney, 58n21, 129n11
Stein, Edith, 83n13
Steinem, Gloria, 85
Storkey, Elaine, 12n2, 25n9, 71n32,
    81n8, 88n23, 92n28, 124
Strauss, Mark, 117
Swartley, William M., 13n4, 105n1

Tertullian, 25n9, 107
Thatcher, Margaret, 26
theology, 30, 17n2
  history of, 32
  and intuition, 28, 112–13
  and method, 23–24, 28, 30–32,
    52n13, 75–77, 101–2, 106
  and social practice, 28
  See also feminism: and theology
Tinder, Glenn, 97n33
Tracy, David, 124
tradition, 9, 15, 27, 107, 111–12
traditionalists. *See* complementarians
Trible, Phyllis, 12n3, 124
Trinity, 76–77
Tucker, Ruth A., 112n3

Van Leeuwen, Mary Stewart, 18–
    19n4, 25n8, 71n32, 88n23, 105n1,
    124
vocation, principle of, 50, 97–98, 101

Watson, Natalie K., 127–28n10

Webb, William J., 10–11n1, 39–41,
  56n19, 71–72n33, 81–82n11,
  89n26, 105n1
Wesley, John, 107
Wesleyan Quadrilateral, 27, 30–32,
  72, 107–12
  and experience, 22, 84, 86–97
  and reason, 77, 80
  and tradition, 15, 27, 34, 72, 85,
  107, 111–12, 123–25
  See also Bible: interpretation of
Wilcox, W. Bradford, 61n23
Wilson, Jonathan, 13n4
Wolters, Clifton, 41n8
Wolterstorff, Nicholas, 103n35
women
  and church, 29, 37, 51, 67

and covering of heads, 29
and equality, 16, 48, 51
and leadership, 26, 34, 54–55, 57,
  70, 80, 82–84
and prophecy, 29, 53
and scholarship, 124
and submission, 16, 59, 63, 69, 72,
  78–79
and subordination, 13n4, 24–25, 53
and work, 91

Yoder, John Howard, 13n4, 42–43n9,
  62n24
Young, Pamela Dickey, 105, 106n2

Scripture Index

Genesis

1 66, 67, 77, 88
1:26–27 35, 66
2 35, 66, 67, 68n29, 88
2:18–24 35
2:24 59
3 36, 37, 42, 82n12

Exodus

21 66

Leviticus

12:1–5 63
12:6–7 65–66
15 63

Deuteronomy

32:11 120

1 Samuel

3:10 103

2 Samuel

1:19–27 125

Psalms

1 118
19:7–9 108–109

Isaiah

7:14 116
40:3–4 39
53 125
55:9 39
62:5 122

Matthew

5:31–32 33
15:14 82
19:3–9 64–65
22:40 29
23:37 120

Mark

15:40–41 36

Luke

1:38 103
8:1–3 36
10:38–42 36

John

4 36
11:1–44 36
12:1–8 36

Acts

2:16–18 36
15 29, 50
15:23–29 34

Romans

5:17 46
6:23 46
8:2 46
8:32 41
12:6–8 36
12:18–13:12 43–44
14:12–13 102
14:14–23 34
16 67
16:1 54
16:1–12 36
16:7 54

1 Corinthians

1:18–31   107
7:20–24   44
7:31   44
7:32   42n9
8   34
8:12–13   47
10:23–24   47
10:25–30   34
11   52n13
11–14   49
11:1–10   50
11:3–7   53
11:7–10   66
11:10   66
11:11–12   68
12:8–10   36
12:27–30   36
12:28   55n15
14   21
14:6   55n15
14:26   51
14:33–35   29, 37, 52
14:34–35   50

Galatians

1:3–5   46
3:26–28   46
3:28   29, 36
5:13–14   47

Ephesians

4:11   36
5   59, 60, 68, 78
5:16   46
5:21   69

5:21–33   59–60
5:21–6:9   58
5:22   69
5:22–33   50
5:25   122
5:29   122
6   29
6:1–4   50
6:5–9   50

Philippians

2:3–8   48–49

Colossians

1:24   41
3   29
3:18–19   50
3:18–22   57–58
3:20–21   50
3:22–25   50
3:25   58n20
4:1   58, 58n20
4:5   46

1 Thessalonians

4:10–12   43
4:13–5:3   42

1 Timothy

2   52n13
2:1–4   53
2:11–12   29, 37, 50
2:11–14   82
2:11–15   23, 52n13, 53,
   68n29
2:13–14   67

2:14   67
3:4–5   50
3:12   50
5:3–16   68n29
5:17   50
6:1   44
6:1–2   50

2 Timothy

3:16   65

Titus

2:4–5   63
2:9–10   44, 50

Hebrews

2:14–15   46
10:24   102

1 Peter

2   29
2:12–17   44–45
2:16   47
2:18   50
2:18–3:7   58
3:1–2   63
3:1–7   50, 69–70
3:7   62
5:1–5   50

1 John

2:2   116
4:10   116